Sunday
DINNERS

RDA ENTHUSIAST BRANDS, LLC
MILWAUKEE, WI

PAGE 11

PAGE 67

PAGE 94

PAGE 105

Sunday
DINNERS

EDITORIAL
EDITOR-IN-CHIEF Catherine Cassidy
**VICE PRESIDENT, CONTENT
 OPERATIONS** Kerri Balliet
CREATIVE DIRECTOR Howard Greenberg

**MANAGING EDITOR, PRINT & DIGITAL
 BOOKS** Mark Hagen
ASSOCIATE CREATIVE DIRECTOR
 Edwin Robles Jr.

ASSOCIATE EDITOR Molly Jasinski
GRAPHIC DESIGNER Courtney Lovetere
LAYOUT DESIGNER Sophie Beck
EDITORIAL SERVICES MANAGER
 Dena Ahlers
EDITORIAL PRODUCTION COORDINATOR
 Jill Banks
COPY CHIEF Deb Warlaumont Mulvey
COPY EDITORS Dulcie Shoener (senior),
 Ronald Kovach, Chris McLaughlin, Ellie Piper

CONTENT DIRECTOR Julie Blume Benedict
FOOD EDITORS Gina Nistico; James Schend;
 Peggy Woodward, RDN
RECIPE EDITORS Sue Ryon (lead), Irene Yeh
EDITORIAL SERVICES ADMINISTRATOR
 Marie Brannon

CULINARY DIRECTOR Sarah Thompson
TEST COOKS Nicholas Iverson (lead),
 Matthew Hass
FOOD STYLISTS Kathryn Conrad (lead),
 Lauren Knoelke, Shannon Roum
PREP COOKS Bethany Van Jacobson (lead),
 Aria C. Thornton
CULINARY TEAM ASSISTANT
 Maria Petrella

PHOTOGRAPHY DIRECTOR
 Stephanie Marchese
PHOTOGRAPHERS Dan Roberts,
 Jim Wieland
PHOTOGRAPHER/SET STYLIST
 Grace Natoli Sheldon
SET STYLISTS Melissa Franco (lead),
 Stacey Genaw, Dee Dee Schaefer
SET STYLIST ASSISTANT
 Stephanie Chojnacki

**BUSINESS ARCHITECT, PUBLISHING
 TECHNOLOGIES** Amanda Harmatys
**BUSINESS ANALYST, PUBLISHING
 TECHNOLOGIES** Kate Unger
**JUNIOR BUSINESS ANALYST,
 PUBLISHING TECHNOLOGIES**
 Shannon Stroud

EDITORIAL BUSINESS MANAGER
 Kristy Martin
EDITORIAL BUSINESS ASSOCIATE
 Andrea Meiers

EDITOR, *TASTE OF HOME* Emily Betz Tyra
ART DIRECTOR, *TASTE OF HOME*
 Kristin Bowker

BUSINESS
PUBLISHER, *TASTE OF HOME*
 Donna Lindskog
**BUSINESS DEVELOPMENT DIRECTOR,
 TASTE OF HOME LIVE** Laurel Osman

**STRATEGIC PARTNERSHIPS MANAGER,
 TASTE OF HOME LIVE**
 Jamie Piette Andrzejewski

TRUSTED MEDIA BRANDS, INC.
**PRESIDENT & CHIEF EXECUTIVE
 OFFICER** Bonnie Kintzer
CHIEF FINANCIAL OFFICER Dean Durbin
CHIEF MARKETING OFFICER C. Alec Casey
CHIEF REVENUE OFFICER Richard Sutton
CHIEF DIGITAL OFFICER Vince Errico
**SENIOR VICE PRESIDENT, GLOBAL HR
 & COMMUNICATIONS**
 Phyllis E. Gebhardt, SPHR; SHRM-SCP
GENERAL COUNSEL Mark Sirota
VICE PRESIDENT, PRODUCT MARKETING
 Brian Kennedy
**VICE PRESIDENT, CONSUMER
 ACQUISITION** Heather Plant
VICE PRESIDENT, OPERATIONS
 Michael Garzone
**VICE PRESIDENT, CONSUMER
 MARKETING PLANNING** Jim Woods
**VICE PRESIDENT, DIGITAL PRODUCT
 & TECHNOLOGY** Nick Contardo
**VICE PRESIDENT, DIGITAL CONTENT &
 AUDIENCE DEVELOPMENT** Kari Hodes
**VICE PRESIDENT, FINANCIAL PLANNING
 & ANALYSIS** William Houston

COVER PHOTOGRAPHY
PHOTOGRAPHER Grace Natoli Sheldon
FOOD STYLIST Kathryn Conrad
SET STYLIST Dee Dee Schaefer

PICTURED ON THE FRONT COVER:
Beef Potato Meat Loaf, page 9
Orange Spice Carrots, page 57
Jeweled Endive Salad, page 42
Easy Cheesy Biscuits, page 76
Mudslide Cheesecake, page 83

PICTURED ON THE TITLE PAGE:
Ribbon Salad with Orange Vinaigrette, page 50
Sunday Roast Chicken, page 21
Chocolate S'mores Tart, page 87

PICTURED ON THE BACK COVER:
Puff Pastry Chicken Potpie, page 35
Summer Orzo, page 61
Berry & Ganache Cheesecake Bars, page 89

TIME FOR FAMILY & FOOD

Some of our best memories center around family and food. That's why we've put together a cookbook devoted entirely to special meals to share with your loved ones—*Taste of Home Sunday Dinners*.

To start off, choose from hearty entree options, such as **Pan-Roasted Chicken & Vegetables (p. 15)** or **Grandma's Cajun Chicken & Spaghetti (p. 23).** If you're in more of a casserole mood, see **Ham & Veggie Casserole (p. 27)** or **Baked Simple Meatball Stroganoff (p. 37).**

From there, you can mix and match recipes to create the perfect dinner. Want something light? Pick winners like **Spinach Salad with Poppy Seed Dressing (p. 50)** or **Roasted Green Beans with Lemon & Walnuts (p. 62).** Need a cozy soup and bread combination? Look no further than **The Ultimate Chicken Noodle Soup (p. 70)** and **Cheese-Filled Garlic Rolls (p. 81).**

In addition, flip through the Sunday Extras chapter to start the fun early with delicious appetizers and beverages. Choose from instant favorites such as **Slow Cooker Spinach & Artichoke Dip (p. 101)** and **Fresh-Squeezed Pink Lemonade (p. 99).**

For the grand finale, bring out a stunning dessert. Take a sweet after-dinner detour with **Orange Dream Mini Cupcakes (p. 97)** or **Easy Lemon Pie (p. 84),** or perhaps cool down with **New York-Style Cheesecake Mousse (p. 87).**

We've included **three special icons** throughout this book to make it easy for you to find just what you're looking for, whether it's a recipe with a handful of ingredients or a meal you can have on the table with minimum fuss. Check out:

> **FAST FIX** Done in 30 minutes or less
> **⑤ INGREDIENTS** 5 ingredients max, plus staples like salt, pepper and oil
> **SLOW COOKER** 🍲 Set it and forget it

You'll also find conversation starters inside to get everyone talking. Questions like "Do you have a favorite vacation memory?" are sure to get great reactions!

Start a new tradition! Whatever day of the week you choose, *Taste of Home Sunday Dinners* is here to help create lasting memories, starting with the food you love.

◇◇◇◇◇◇◇◇◇◇◇◇◇◇◇◇◇◇◇◇◇◇◇◇◇◇◇◇◇◇◇◇◇◇◇

GET SOCIAL WITH US!

 LIKE US
facebook.com/
tasteofhome

 PIN US
pinterest.com/
taste_of_home

 FOLLOW US
@tasteofhome

TWEET US
twitter.com/
tasteofhome

To find a recipe
tasteofhome.com

To submit a recipe
tasteofhome.com/submit

To find out about other
Taste of Home products
shoptasteofhome.com

PAGE 41

PAGE 76

Table Talk!

Make your time at the table as memorable as possible! Consider the following conversation starters, and liven up family meals at your home. Give them a try and see just how fun dinnertime can be!

◇◇◇◇◇◇◇◇◇◇◇◇◇◇◇◇◇◇◇◇

Who is your all-time favorite athlete?

Why is that person your favorite? What makes them stand out from the crowd? Share a highlight you love from that athlete's career and why it's so memorable.

What is the best concert you ever saw? Why was it so special?

Everyone remembers the first concert they saw. What was yours? Was that the best concert you've ever attended? If not, what was?

What is the best gift you've ever received?

Was it for Christmas, your birthday or something else? Why did it mean so much to you?

If you could only eat one dessert for the rest of your life, what would it be?

Life is sweetest with dessert, but what if you had to choose one? Share with your family why your choice is tops.

What is your favorite movie?

Yes, you have to choose one! Why is it your favorite? Do you have a line from the movie that you use often in life? Who is the best character in the film?

Do you have a favorite vacation memory?

Whether they're a delightful getaway or perhaps a comedy of errors, vacations have a way of creating the best moments! Discuss everyone's favorite and why that particular trip stands out.

If you could be an Olympian, which sport would you compete in?

Dream big! You can choose any sport from the summer or winter games! What about that particular sport makes it so appealing to you?

If you could start a new hobby, what would it be?

Think of a skill or activity you've always been interested in but just haven't taken the time to try out. Does anyone in your family have a similar interest? Discuss a first step you can take to get involved with this new hobby.

Who is your personal hero?

It can be someone famous or someone you know in everyday life. Why is that person so important to you? In what ways have they inspired you?

Discuss a time you laughed so hard you cried.

We all love to laugh, right? Tell everyone at the table about the time you laughed the hardest. What made that moment so funny?

What is your all-time favorite meal?

We're talking best of the best here! Was it a meal prepared by Mom, Grandma or someone else? What makes it so memorable? Have you tried re-creating it yourself?

BALSAMIC ROAST
CHICKEN

Main Dishes

You know what brings people together? Comforting, homemade food! Serve your loved ones the best of the best when you choose one of the savory entrees that follow.

BALSAMIC ROAST CHICKEN

When the aroma from this dish fills your house, your family will think you spent all day cooking. But this elegant, Sunday-special entree, flavored with rosemary, wine and balsamic vinegar, is surprisingly simple to make.

—**TRACY TYLKOWSKI** OMAHA, NE

PREP: 20 MIN. • **BAKE:** 2 HOURS + STANDING
MAKES: 12 SERVINGS (1½ CUPS ONION SAUCE)

- 2 tablespoons minced fresh rosemary or 2 teaspoons dried rosemary, crushed
- 3 garlic cloves, minced
- 1 teaspoon salt
- 1 teaspoon pepper
- 2 medium red onions, chopped
- 1 roasting chicken (6 to 7 pounds)
- ½ cup dry red wine or reduced-sodium chicken broth
- ½ cup balsamic vinegar

1. Preheat oven to 350°. Mix rosemary, garlic, salt and pepper. Place onions in a roasting pan; place chicken over onions, breast side up.
2. Pat chicken dry. With fingers, carefully loosen skin from chicken; rub rosemary mixture under the skin. Secure skin to underside of breast with toothpicks. Tuck wings under chicken; tie drumsticks together.
3. Mix wine and vinegar; pour over chicken. Roast until a thermometer inserted in thickest part of thigh reads 170°-175°, 2-2½ hours. (Cover loosely with foil if chicken browns too quickly.)
4. Remove chicken from oven; tent with foil. Let stand 15 minutes before carving. Transfer onion and pan drippings to a small bowl; skim fat. Remove and discard skin from chicken before serving. Serve with onion sauce.

FAST FIX ▶
APPLE-CHERRY PORK MEDALLIONS

If you're too busy to cook, my pork medallions with tangy apple-cherry sauce, fresh rosemary and thyme deliver the goods in a hurry.

—**GLORIA BRADLEY** NAPERVILLE, IL

START TO FINISH: 30 MIN.
MAKES: 4 SERVINGS

- 1 pork tenderloin (1 pound)
- 1 teaspoon minced fresh rosemary or ¼ teaspoon dried rosemary, crushed
- 1 teaspoon minced fresh thyme or ¼ teaspoon dried thyme
- ½ teaspoon celery salt
- 1 tablespoon olive oil
- 1 large apple, sliced
- ⅔ cup unsweetened apple juice
- 3 tablespoons dried tart cherries
- 1 tablespoon honey
- 1 tablespoon cider vinegar
- 1 package (8.8 ounces) ready-to-serve brown rice

1. Cut the tenderloin crosswise into 12 slices; sprinkle with rosemary, thyme and celery salt. In a large nonstick skillet, heat oil over medium-high heat. Brown pork on both sides; remove from pan.
2. In the same skillet, combine the apple, apple juice, cherries, honey and vinegar. Bring to a boil, stirring to loosen browned bits from pan. Reduce heat; simmer, uncovered, 3-4 minutes or just until apple is tender.
3. Return pork to pan, turning to coat with sauce; cook, covered, 3-4 minutes or until pork is tender. Meanwhile, prepare rice according to package directions; serve with pork mixture.

TEST KITCHEN TIP
You can save fresh rosemary for later by freezing it for up to three months. Frozen rosemary has a stronger flavor than fresh, though, so you may want to use slightly less than what your recipe calls for.

**BEEF POTATO
MEAT LOAF**
Christina Addison
Blanchester, OH

BEEF POTATO MEAT LOAF

I've watched the film *A Christmas Story* so many times since I was a kid. Now that I have a family of my own, I re-created the mom's meat loaf and mashed potatoes from that movie.

—CHRISTINA ADDISON BLANCHESTER, OH

PREP: 15 MIN. • **BAKE:** 50 MIN. + STANDING
MAKES: 6 SERVINGS

- 2 **large eggs, lightly beaten**
- ½ **cup ketchup**
- 1 **medium onion, finely chopped**
- 1 **small green or sweet red pepper, finely chopped**
- ⅔ **cup crushed saltines (about 12)**
- ½ **teaspoon salt**
- 1 **teaspoon pepper**
- 1½ **pounds ground beef**
- 4 **cups hot mashed potatoes, divided**
- 1 **tablespoon minced fresh parsley**

1. Preheat oven to 375°. Place a rack in a 15x10x1-in. baking pan; place a 12x8-in. piece of foil in center of rack. In a large bowl, combine the eggs, ketchup, onion, green pepper, crushed saltines, salt and pepper. Add beef; mix lightly but thoroughly. Place over foil rectangle and shape into a 9x6-in. loaf. Bake until a thermometer reads 160°, 50-60 minutes. Let stand 10 minutes before slicing.
2. Transfer meat loaf to a serving plate, discarding the foil. Pipe or spread 1 cup mashed potatoes over meat loaf. Sprinkle with parsley. Serve with remaining mashed potatoes.

GOES GREAT WITH

Serve Orange Spice Carrots, page 57, with meat loaf to create the ultimate cozy dinner.

COUNTRY RIBS DINNER

SLOW COOKER
COUNTRY RIBS DINNER

This is my favorite recipe for a classic ribs dinner. It's always a treat for my family when we have this.

—ROSE INGALL MANISTEE, MI

PREP: 10 MIN. • **COOK:** 6¼ HOURS
MAKES: 4 SERVINGS

- 2 **pounds boneless country-style pork ribs**
- ½ **teaspoon salt**
- ¼ **teaspoon pepper**
- 8 **small red potatoes (about 1 pound), halved**
- 4 **medium carrots, cut into 1-inch pieces**
- 3 **celery ribs, cut into ½-inch pieces**
- 1 **medium onion, coarsely chopped**
- ¾ **cup water**
- 1 **garlic clove, crushed**
- 1 **can (10¾ ounces) condensed cream of mushroom soup, undiluted**

1. Sprinkle the ribs with salt and pepper; transfer to a 4-qt. slow cooker. Add potatoes, carrots, celery, onion, water and garlic. Cook, covered, on low until meat and vegetables are tender, 6-8 hours.
2. Remove meat and vegetables; skim fat from cooking juices. Whisk soup into cooking juices; return meat and vegetables to slow cooker. Cook, covered, until heated through, 15-30 minutes longer.

MY MOM'S BEST MEAT LOAF

The Rice Krispies used in this recipe are my mom's secret ingredient. While they may seem odd, they help hold the meat loaf together. Once cooked, no one realizes they were even there.

—**KELLY SIMMONS** HOPKINSVILLE, KY

PREP: 10 MIN. • **BAKE:** 1 HOUR + STANDING
MAKES: 8 SERVINGS

- ½ cup chili sauce
- ¼ cup ketchup
- 2 cups Rice Krispies
- 1 medium onion, finely chopped
- 1 small green or sweet red pepper, finely chopped
- ¾ cup shredded part-skim mozzarella cheese
- 1 large egg, lightly beaten
- ½ teaspoon salt
- ¼ teaspoon pepper
- 2 pounds ground beef

1. Preheat oven to 350°. In a small bowl, mix chili sauce and ketchup. In a large bowl, combine Rice Krispies, onion, green pepper, cheese, egg, salt and pepper; stir in half of the chili sauce mixture. Add beef; mix lightly but thoroughly.

2. Transfer beef mixture to an ungreased 9x5-in. loaf pan. Make a shallow indentation down center of loaf. Spread remaining chili sauce mixture over loaf, being sure to fill indentation.

3. Bake until a thermometer reads 160°, 60-70 minutes; use a turkey baster to remove the drippings every 20 minutes. Let stand 10 minutes before slicing.

NOTE *This recipe was tested with Heinz chili sauce.*

HERB-ROASTED SALMON FILLETS

⑤ INGREDIENTS FAST FIX
HERB-ROASTED SALMON FILLETS

Roasted salmon is so simple to prepare, yet elegant enough to serve to company. I make it on days when I have less than an hour to cook.

—**LUANNE ASTA** EAST HAMPTON, NY

START TO FINISH: 30 MIN.
MAKES: 4 SERVINGS

- 4 salmon fillets (6 ounces each)
- 4 garlic cloves, minced
- 1 tablespoon minced fresh rosemary or 1 teaspoon dried rosemary, crushed
- 1 tablespoon olive oil
- 2 teaspoons minced fresh thyme or ½ teaspoon dried thyme
- ¾ teaspoon salt
- ½ teaspoon pepper

Preheat oven to 425°. Place salmon in a greased 15x10x1-in. baking pan, skin side down. Combine the remaining ingredients; spread over fillets. Roast to desired doneness, 15-18 minutes.

TEST KITCHEN TIP
Buying fresh salmon from the store? Store it in the coolest part of your refrigerator for one to two days max after bringing it home.

SLOW COOKER TURKEY PESTO LASAGNA

My cheesy, noodle-y lasagna makes any slow cooker skeptic a believer. I'll usually bring more pesto and marinara to the table for our resident sauce lovers.
—**BLAIR LONERGAN** ROCHELLE, VA

PREP: 25 MIN.
COOK: 3 HOURS + STANDING
MAKES: 8 SERVINGS

- 1 **pound ground turkey**
- 1 **small onion, chopped**
- 2 **teaspoons Italian seasoning**
- ½ **teaspoon salt**
- 2 **cups (8 ounces) shredded part-skim mozzarella cheese, divided**
- 1 **container (15 ounces) whole-milk ricotta cheese**
- ¼ **cup prepared pesto**
- 1 **jar (24 ounces) marinara sauce**
- 9 **no-cook lasagna noodles Grated Parmesan cheese**

1. Cut three 25x3-in. strips of heavy-duty foil; crisscross so they resemble spokes of a wheel. Place strips on bottom and up sides of a greased 5-qt. slow cooker. Coat strips with cooking spray.

2. In a large skillet, cook turkey and onion over medium heat 6-8 minutes or until turkey is no longer pink, breaking up turkey into crumbles; drain. Stir in Italian seasoning and salt.

3. In a bowl, mix 1 cup mozzarella cheese, ricotta cheese and pesto. In the prepared slow cooker, layer a third of each of the following: marinara sauce, noodles (breaking noodles if necessary to fit), turkey mixture and cheese mixture. Repeat the layers twice. Sprinkle with remaining mozzarella cheese.

4. Cook, covered, on low until noodles are tender, 3-4 hours. Turn off slow cooker; remove insert. Let stand, uncovered, 30 minutes before serving. Using foil strips, remove lasagna to a platter. Serve with Parmesan cheese.

SLOW COOKER TURKEY PESTO LASAGNA

BUTTERNUT SQUASH, CAULIFLOWER & BEEF SHEPHERD'S PIE

I love to get creative with classic dishes, such as this colorful version of shepherd's pie. Adding squash and cauliflower boosts the nutritional value and cuts the calories.
—**JENN TIDWELL** FAIR OAKS, CA

PREP: 50 MIN. • **BAKE:** 35 MIN. + STANDING
MAKES: 6 SERVINGS

- 4 **tablespoons butter, melted and divided**
- 2 **tablespoons maple syrup Dash pepper**
- 1 **medium butternut squash (about 2½ pounds), peeled and cubed**
- 1 **tablespoon minced fresh thyme or 1 teaspoon dried thyme**
- 1¼ **pounds ground beef**
- 1 **envelope onion soup mix**
- 1 **cup water**
- 1 **medium head cauliflower, broken into small florets**
- 4 **garlic cloves, minced**
- 1 **cup freshly grated Parmesan cheese**

1. Preheat oven to 350°. Combine 2 tablespoons melted butter, syrup and pepper; toss with the squash to coat. Roast squash in a greased 15x10x1-in. baking pan until tender, 40-45 minutes. Transfer to a large bowl; mash squash until smooth, stirring in thyme.

2. In a large skillet over medium heat, cook and stir beef, crumbling meat, until no longer pink, 6-8 minutes; drain. Stir in soup mix and water; bring to a boil. Reduce heat; simmer, uncovered, until slightly thickened, 4-6 minutes. Transfer to a greased 13x9-in. baking dish.

3. Top evenly with cauliflower. Sprinkle with garlic; drizzle with remaining butter. Spread squash mixture over top. Bake, uncovered, until cauliflower is tender, 35-40 minutes. Sprinkle with cheese. Let stand 10 minutes before serving.

ALFREDO-PANCETTA STUFFED SHELLS

I thought up this recipe while I was driving home from work. The local paper started a new reader recipe feature, so I sent this in, and I was published! Warm up some bread, pour the chardonnay and enjoy.
—**TAMI VOLTZ** RUDOLPH, OH

PREP: 30 MIN. • **BAKE:** 35 MIN.
MAKES: 6 SERVINGS

- 12 uncooked jumbo pasta shells
- 4 ounces pancetta, finely chopped
- 1 teaspoon olive oil
- 1 package (6 ounces) fresh baby spinach
- 2 garlic cloves, minced
- ½ teaspoon crushed red pepper flakes
- 1 carton (15 ounces) part-skim ricotta cheese
- 2 tablespoons grated Parmesan cheese
- 1 large egg yolk, beaten
- ¼ teaspoon pepper
- 1 jar (15 ounces) roasted garlic Alfredo sauce
- ½ cup shredded mozzarella cheese

1. Cook pasta shells according to package directions; drain and rinse with cold water.

2. Meanwhile, cook the pancetta in oil in a large skillet over medium heat until crisp. Remove to paper towels, reserving drippings. Saute spinach, garlic and pepper flakes in drippings until spinach is wilted.

3. Transfer spinach mixture to a small bowl. Add ricotta, Parmesan cheese, egg yolk and pepper; mix well.

4. Spread ½ cup Alfredo sauce into a greased 11x7-in. baking dish. Spoon ricotta mixture into pasta shells; place in baking dish. Pour remaining sauce over shells.

5. Cover and bake at 375° for 25 minutes. Sprinkle with mozzarella cheese. Bake until the cheese is melted, 10-15 minutes longer. Top with pancetta.

BEEF & BACON GNOCCHI SKILLET

FAST FIX
BEEF & BACON GNOCCHI SKILLET

My husband's favorite meal—a bacon cheeseburger—inspired me to create this amazing gnocchi dish. Top it as you would a burger—with ketchup, mustard and pickles.
—**ASHLEY LECKER** GREEN BAY, WI

START TO FINISH: 30 MIN.
MAKES: 6 SERVINGS

- 1 package (16 ounces) potato gnocchi
- 1¼ pounds lean ground beef (90% lean)
- 1 medium onion, chopped
- 8 cooked bacon strips, crumbled and divided
- 1 cup water
- ½ cup heavy whipping cream
- 1 tablespoon ketchup
- ¼ teaspoon salt
- ¼ teaspoon pepper
- 1½ cups shredded cheddar cheese
- ½ cup chopped tomatoes
- 2 green onions, sliced

1. Preheat broiler. Cook gnocchi according to package directions; drain.

2. Meanwhile, in a large ovenproof skillet, cook the beef and onion, crumbling beef, over medium heat until no longer pink, about 4-6 minutes. Drain.

3. Stir in half of bacon; add the gnocchi, water, cream and ketchup. Bring to a boil. Cook, stirring, over medium heat until sauce has thickened, 3-4 minutes. Add seasonings. Sprinkle with cheese.

4. Broil 3-4 in. from heat until cheese has melted, 1-2 minutes. Top with tomatoes, green onions and remaining bacon.

NOTE *Look for potato gnocchi in the pasta or frozen foods section.*

MAPLE-SAGE BRINED TURKEY

We use maple-sage brine to help brown the turkey and make the meat incredibly juicy and delicious.

—**KIMBERLY FORNI** LACONIA, NH

PREP: 40 MIN. + BRINING
BAKE: 2½ HOURS + STANDING
MAKES: 20 SERVINGS

- 4 quarts water
- 1½ cups packed brown sugar
- 1 cup sea salt
- 1 cup maple syrup
- 1 cup cider vinegar
- 24 fresh sage leaves
- 6 bay leaves
- 2 tablespoons yellow mustard
- 2 tablespoons coarsely ground pepper
- 1 teaspoon ground cloves
- 4 quarts ice water
- 2 turkey-size oven roasting bags
- 1 turkey (14 to 16 pounds)

TURKEY
- 2 tablespoons olive oil
- ½ teaspoon pepper
- ½ teaspoon salt, optional

1. In a large stockpot, combine the first 10 ingredients; bring to a boil. Cook and stir until sugar and salt are dissolved. Remove from the heat. Add 4 quarts ice water to cool the brine to room temperature.

2. Put one turkey-sized oven roasting bag inside the other; place in a large stockpot. Place turkey inside both bags; pour in cooled brine. Seal bags, pressing out as much air as possible. Refrigerate 18-24 hours.

3. Preheat oven to 350°. Remove turkey from brine; rinse and pat dry. Discard brine. Place turkey on a rack in a shallow roasting pan, breast side up. Tuck wings under turkey; tie drumsticks together. Rub oil over outside of turkey; sprinkle with pepper and, if desired, salt.

4. Roast turkey, uncovered, until a thermometer inserted in thickest part of thigh reads 170°-175°, 2½-3 hours. (Cover loosely with foil if the turkey browns too quickly.)

5. Remove turkey from oven; tent with foil. Let stand turkey 20 minutes before carving.

**MAPLE-SAGE
BRINED TURKEY**

PAN-ROASTED CHICKEN & VEGETABLES

This one-dish meal tastes like it needs hours of hands-on time to put together, but it's just minutes to prep the simple ingredients. So easy.

—**SHERRI MELOTIK** OAK CREEK, WI

PREP: 15 MIN. • **BAKE:** 45 MIN.
MAKES: 6 SERVINGS

- 2 **pounds red potatoes (about 6 medium), cut into ¾-inch pieces**
- 1 **large onion, coarsely chopped**
- 2 **tablespoons olive oil**
- 3 **garlic cloves, minced**
- 1¼ **teaspoons salt, divided**
- 1 **teaspoon dried rosemary, crushed, divided**
- ¾ **teaspoon pepper, divided**
- ½ **teaspoon paprika**
- 6 **bone-in chicken thighs (about 2¼ pounds), skin removed**
- 6 **cups fresh baby spinach (about 6 ounces)**

1. Preheat oven to 425°. In a large bowl, combine potatoes, onion, oil, garlic, ¾ teaspoon salt, ½ teaspoon rosemary and ½ teaspoon pepper; toss to coat. Transfer to a 15x10x1-in. baking pan coated with cooking spray.

2. In a small bowl, mix paprika and the remaining salt, rosemary and pepper. Sprinkle chicken with the paprika mixture; arrange over vegetables. Roast until a thermometer inserted in chicken reads 170°-175° and vegetables are just tender, 35-40 minutes.

3. Remove chicken to a serving platter; keep warm. Top vegetables with spinach. Roast until vegetables are tender and spinach is wilted, 8-10 minutes longer. Stir vegetables to combine; serve with chicken.

TEST KITCHEN TIP
You can stop crying over chopped onions! Before chopping, try freezing the onion for about 20 minutes to cut back on the tears.

COFFEE-BRAISED ROAST BEEF

SLOW COOKER
COFFEE-BRAISED ROAST BEEF

This recipe has been a family tradition since 1974. The coffee adds an intriguing flavor to the roast, and the juices can be thickened for a delicious gravy.

—**NANCY SCHULER** BELLE FOURCHE, SD

PREP: 10 MIN. + MARINATING
COOK: 6½ HOURS
MAKES: 10 SERVINGS

- 1 **cup cider vinegar**
- 4 **garlic cloves, crushed, divided**
- 1 **boneless beef chuck roast (4 to 5 pounds), trimmed**
- 2 **teaspoons salt**
- 1 **teaspoon pepper**
- 1 **cup strong brewed coffee**
- 1 **cup beef broth**
- 1 **medium onion, sliced**
- 3 **tablespoons cornstarch**
- ¼ **cup cold water**
  Mashed potatoes

1. In a large resealable plastic bag, combine vinegar and 2 garlic cloves. Add roast; seal bag and turn to coat. Refrigerate overnight, turning occasionally.

2. Drain and discard marinade. Pat roast dry; sprinkle with salt and pepper. Place roast in a 5- or 6-qt. slow cooker; add coffee, broth, onion and remaining garlic. Cook, covered, on low until meat is tender, 6-7 hours.

3. Remove roast and keep warm. Strain cooking juices, discarding onion and garlic; skim fat. In a small bowl, mix cornstarch and cold water until smooth; gradually stir into the slow cooker. Cook, covered, on high until gravy is thickened, 30 minutes. Slice the roast; serve with mashed potatoes and gravy.

MELT-IN-YOUR-MOUTH CHUCK ROAST

My husband and I sometimes vary the heat in this recipe with Cajun seasoning and green chilies. You'll love how flavorful and tender this comforting roast turns out. Shred any leftovers and use the gravy as a base for soup—it's terrific.
—**BETTE McCUMBER** SCHENECTADY, NY

PREP: 20 MIN. • **COOK:** 5 HOURS
MAKES: 6 SERVINGS

- 1 can (14½ ounces) Italian stewed tomatoes, undrained
- ½ cup beef broth
- ½ cup ketchup
- 3 tablespoons brown sugar
- 2 tablespoons Worcestershire sauce
- 4 teaspoons prepared mustard
- 3 garlic cloves, minced
- 1 tablespoon soy sauce
- 2 teaspoons pepper
- ¼ teaspoon crushed red pepper flakes
- 1 large onion, halved and sliced
- 1 medium green pepper, halved and sliced
- 1 celery rib, chopped
- 1 boneless beef chuck roast (2 to 3 pounds)
- 3 tablespoons cornstarch
- ¼ cup cold water

1. Mix the first 10 ingredients. Place onion, green pepper and celery in a 5-qt. slow cooker; place roast over top. Pour tomato mixture over roast. Cook, covered, on low until meat is tender, 5-6 hours.

2. Remove roast. Strain cooking juices, reserving vegetables. Transfer juices to a small saucepan; skim fat. Mix cornstarch and water until smooth; stir into cooking juices. Bring to a boil; cook and stir until thickened, 1-2 minutes. Serve the roast and vegetables with gravy.

FREEZE OPTION *Place sliced beef and vegetables in freezer containers; top with gravy. Cool and freeze. To use, partially thaw in the refrigerator overnight. Heat through slowly in a covered saucepan, stirring gently and adding a little broth or water if necessary.*

TURKEY SAUSAGE-STUFFED ACORN SQUASH

TURKEY SAUSAGE-STUFFED ACORN SQUASH

Finding healthy recipes the family will eat is a challenge. This elegant squash is one we love, and it works with pork, turkey and chicken sausage.
—**MELISSA PELKEY HASS** WALESKA, GA

PREP: 30 MIN. • **BAKE:** 50 MIN.
MAKES: 8 SERVINGS

- 4 medium acorn squash (about 1½ pounds each)
- 1 cup cherry tomatoes, halved
- 1 pound Italian turkey sausage links, casings removed
- ½ pound sliced fresh mushrooms
- 1 medium apple, peeled and finely chopped
- 1 small onion, finely chopped
- 2 teaspoons fennel seed
- 2 teaspoons caraway seeds
- ½ teaspoon dried sage leaves
- 3 cups fresh baby spinach
- 1 tablespoon minced fresh thyme
- ¼ teaspoon salt
- ⅛ teaspoon pepper
- 8 ounces fresh mozzarella cheese, chopped
- 1 tablespoon red wine vinegar

1. Preheat oven to 400°. Cut the squash lengthwise in half; remove and discard seeds. Using a sharp knife, cut a thin slice from the bottom of each half to allow them to lie flat. Place squash in a shallow roasting pan, hollow side down; add ¼ in. of hot water and halved tomatoes. Bake, uncovered, 45 minutes.

2. Meanwhile, in a large skillet, cook sausage, mushrooms, apple, onion and dried seasonings over medium heat 8-10 minutes or until sausage is no longer pink, breaking up sausage into crumbles; drain. Add spinach, thyme, salt and pepper; cook and stir 2 minutes. Remove from heat.

3. Carefully remove squash from roasting pan. Drain cooking liquid, reserving tomatoes. Return squash to pan, hollow side up.

4. Stir cheese, vinegar and reserved tomatoes into sausage mixture. Spoon into squash cavities. Bake until heated through and squash is easily pierced with a fork, 5-10 minutes longer.

GINGER HALIBUT WITH BRUSSELS SPROUTS

I moved to the United States from Russia and love cooking Russian food for family and friends. Halibut with soy sauce, ginger and pepper is a favorite.
—**MARGARITA PARKER** NEW BERN, NC

START TO FINISH: 25 MIN.
MAKES: SERVINGS

- 4 **teaspoons lemon juice**
- 4 **halibut fillets (4 to 6 ounces each)**
- 1 **teaspoon minced fresh gingerroot**
- ¼ **to ¾ teaspoon salt, divided**
- ¼ **teaspoon pepper**
- ½ **cup water**
- 10 **ounces (about 2½ cups) fresh Brussels sprouts, halved**
  Crushed red pepper flakes
- 1 **tablespoon canola oil**
- 5 **garlic cloves, sliced lengthwise**
- 2 **tablespoons sesame oil**
- 2 **tablespoons soy sauce**
  Lemon slices, optional

1. Brush lemon juice over halibut fillets. Sprinkle with minced ginger, ¼ teaspoon salt and pepper.
2. Place the fish on an oiled grill rack, skin side down. Grill, covered, over medium heat (or broil 6 in. from heat) until fish just begins to flake easily with a fork, 6-8 minutes.
3. In a large skillet, bring water to a boil over medium-high heat. Add Brussels sprouts, pepper flakes and, if desired, remaining salt. Cook, covered, until tender, 5-7 minutes. Meanwhile, in a small skillet, heat oil over medium heat. Add garlic; cook until golden brown. Drain on paper towels.
4. Drizzle sesame oil and soy sauce over halibut. Serve with Brussels sprouts; sprinkle with fried garlic. If desired, serve with lemon slices.

★ ★ ★ ★ ★ **READER REVIEW**

"I used the broiler to prepare the fish. This is a very unique and easy way to flavor fish. Nice change of pace!"

REMENEC TASTEOFHOME.COM

GINGER HALIBUT WITH BRUSSELS SPROUTS

ARTICHOKE FLORENTINE PASTA

ORANGE-GLAZED PORK WITH SWEET POTATOES

When it's chilly outside, I like to roast pork tenderloin with sweet potatoes, apples and an orange. The sweetness and spices make any evening cozy.

—**DANIELLE LEE BOYLES** WESTON, WI

PREP: 20 MIN. • **BAKE:** 55 MIN. + STANDING
MAKES: 6 SERVINGS

- 1 **pound sweet potatoes (about 2 medium)**
- 2 **medium apples**
- 1 **medium orange**
- 1 **teaspoon salt**
- ½ **teaspoon pepper**
- 1 **cup orange juice**
- 2 **tablespoons brown sugar**
- 2 **teaspoons cornstarch**
- 1 **teaspoon ground cinnamon**
- 1 **teaspoon ground ginger**
- 2 **pork tenderloins (about 1 pound each)**

1. Preheat oven to 350°. Peel sweet potatoes; core apples. Cut potatoes, apples and orange crosswise into ¼-in.-thick slices. Arrange on a foil-lined 15x10x1-in. baking pan coated with cooking spray; sprinkle with salt and pepper. Roast 10 minutes.

2. Meanwhile, in a microwave-safe bowl, mix orange juice, brown sugar, cornstarch, cinnamon and ginger. Microwave, covered, on high, stirring every 30 seconds until thickened, 1-2 minutes. Stir until smooth.

3. Place pork over sweet potato mixture; drizzle with orange juice mixture. Roast until a thermometer inserted in pork reads 145° and the sweet potatoes and apples are tender, 45-55 minutes longer. Remove from oven; tent with foil. Let stand 10 minutes before slicing.

TEST KITCHEN TIP
Once you've cooked sweet potatoes, they'll last for about a week in the refrigerator.

ARTICHOKE FLORENTINE PASTA

Pasta loaded with artichokes and creamy cheese is everything a Sunday dinner should be. Add cooked chicken, shrimp or crab if you like.

—**NANCY BECKMAN** HELENA, MT

PREP: 20 MIN. • **COOK:** 15 MIN.
MAKES: 8 SERVINGS

- 1 **package (16 ounces) penne pasta**
- 6 **tablespoons butter, divided**
- 4 **garlic cloves, minced**
- 12 **ounces fresh baby spinach (about 16 cups)**
- ¼ **cup all-purpose flour**
- 3 **cups 2% milk**
- ¾ **cup grated Parmesan cheese**
- 1 **package (8 ounces) reduced-fat cream cheese**
- ½ **cup white wine or reduced-sodium chicken broth**
- 1 **teaspoon salt**
- ½ **teaspoon pepper**
- ¼ **teaspoon cayenne pepper**
- 2 **cans (14 ounces each) water-packed artichoke hearts, drained and coarsely chopped**
- ⅓ **cup Italian-style panko (Japanese) bread crumbs**

1. Cook the pasta according to package directions. In a 6-qt. Dutch oven, melt 2 tablespoons butter over medium-high heat. Add garlic; cook and stir 30 seconds. Add spinach; cook and stir 1-2 minutes or just until wilted. Remove from pot.

2. In the same pot, melt remaining butter over medium heat. Stir in flour until smooth; gradually whisk in milk. Bring to a boil, stirring constantly; cook and stir 2-3 minutes or until thickened. Add Parmesan cheese, cream cheese, wine and seasonings; stir until smooth. Stir in artichoke hearts; heat through.

3. Drain pasta; add to sauce, tossing to coat. Stir in spinach mixture. Transfer to a serving dish; sprinkle with bread crumbs. Serve immediately.

ORANGE-GLAZED PORK WITH SWEET POTATOES

CITRUS-MOLASSES GLAZED HAM

We are always searching new ways to utilize Florida citrus, which is plentiful during the holidays in our own backyard. This recipe does just that!
—**CHARLENE CHAMBERS** ORMOND BEACH, FL

PREP: 15 MIN. • **BAKE:** 2 HOURS
MAKES: 12 SERVINGS

- 1 **fully cooked bone-in ham (7 to 9 pounds)**

GLAZE
- ½ **cup grapefruit juice**
- ½ **cup orange juice**
- ¼ **cup molasses**
- 3 **tablespoons honey**
- 1 **tablespoon packed brown sugar**
- 1 **tablespoon Dijon mustard**
- 3 **teaspoons coarsely ground pepper**

1. Preheat oven to 325°. Place the ham on a rack in a shallow roasting pan. Using a sharp knife, score surface of ham with ¼-in.-deep cuts in a diamond pattern. Cover and bake 1¾-2¼ hours or until a thermometer reads 130°.

2. Meanwhile, in a large saucepan, combine grapefruit and orange juices. Bring to a boil; cook 6-8 minutes or until liquid is reduced by half. Stir in remaining ingredients; return to a boil. Reduce heat; simmer, uncovered, 12-15 minutes or until thickened.

3. Remove ham from oven. Brush with ⅓ cup glaze. Bake, uncovered, basting occasionally with remaining glaze, until a thermometer reads 140°, 15-20 minutes.

★ ★ ★ ★ ★ **READER REVIEW**

"I made this for our holiday party and everyone loved it. My father-in-law said it was the best ham he has had. My husband liked the light citrus favor."

DANIELLEYLEE TASTEOFHOME.COM

LIGHT & LEMONY SCAMPI

A touch of lemon helped me trim the calories in our favorite shrimp scampi recipe. For those who want to indulge, pass around the Parmesan.
—**ANN SHEEHY** LAWRENCE, MA

PREP: 20 MIN. • **COOK:** 15 MIN.
MAKES: 4 SERVINGS

- 1 **pound uncooked shrimp (26–30 per pound)**
- 8 **ounces uncooked multigrain angel hair pasta**
- 1 **tablespoon butter**
- 1 **tablespoon olive oil**
- 2 **green onions, thinly sliced**
- 4 **garlic cloves, minced**
- ½ **cup reduced-sodium chicken broth**
- 2 **teaspoons grated lemon peel**
- 3 **tablespoons lemon juice**
- ½ **teaspoon freshly ground pepper**
- ¼ **teaspoon salt**
- ¼ **teaspoon crushed red pepper flakes**
- ¼ **cup minced fresh parsley Grated Parmesan cheese, optional**

1. Peel and devein the shrimp, removing tails. Cut each shrimp lengthwise in half. Cook pasta according to package directions.

2. In a large nonstick skillet, heat butter and oil over medium-high heat. Add shrimp, green onions and garlic; cook and stir until shrimp turn pink, 2-3 minutes. Remove from pan with a slotted spoon.

3. Add broth, lemon peel, lemon juice, pepper, salt and pepper flakes to the same pan. Bring to a boil; cook until the liquid is slightly reduced, about 1 minute. Return shrimp to pan; heat through. Remove from heat.

4. Drain pasta; divide among four bowls. Top with shrimp mixture; sprinkle with parsley. If desired, serve with cheese.

LIGHT & LEMONY SCAMPI
Ann Sheehy
Lawrence, MA

SUNDAY ROAST CHICKEN

SUNDAY ROAST CHICKEN

Mixed with orange and lemon juice, my roast chicken is both flavorful and healthy.
—ROBIN HAAS CRANSTON, RI

PREP: 30 MIN. • **BAKE:** 1¾ HOURS + RESTING
MAKES: 6 SERVINGS

- 1 **medium fennel bulb**
- 5 **large carrots, cut into 1½-inch pieces**
- 1 **large white onion, quartered, divided**
- 1 **medium lemon**
- 3 **garlic cloves, minced**
- 1 **tablespoon honey**
- 1 **teaspoon kosher salt**
- 1 **teaspoon crushed red pepper flakes**
- 1 **teaspoon pepper**
- 1 **broiler/fryer chicken (4 pounds)**
- 2 **garlic cloves**
- 1 **cup orange juice**

1. Preheat oven to 350°. Using a sharp knife, trim stalks and root end of fennel bulb. Cut the bulb lengthwise into quarters; cut and remove core. Cut fennel into 1-in. wedges. Place fennel, carrots and three of the onion quarters in a shallow roasting pan, spreading evenly.

2. Cut lemon in half; squeeze juice into a small bowl, reserving lemon halves. Stir minced garlic, honey, salt, pepper flakes and pepper into juice.

3. Place chicken on a work surface, neck side down. With fingers, carefully loosen skin from the tail end of the chicken breast. Spoon juice mixture under skin of breast; secure skin with toothpicks. Place garlic cloves, lemon halves and remaining onion inside chicken cavity. Tuck wings under chicken; tie drumsticks together. Place chicken over the vegetables, breast side up.

4. Pour the orange juice over the chicken. Roast 1½-2 hours or until a thermometer inserted in the thickest part of thigh reads 170°-175°. (Cover loosely with foil if the chicken browns too quickly.)

5. Remove roasting pan from oven; increase oven setting to 450°. Remove chicken from pan; tent with foil and let stand 15 minutes before carving.

6. Meanwhile, return roasting pan to oven; roast vegetables until tender and lightly browned, 10-15 minutes longer. Using a slotted spoon, remove vegetables from pan. If desired, skim fat from pan juices and serve with chicken and vegetables.

FESTIVE SLOW-COOKED BEEF TIPS

We once owned an organic greenhouse and produce business. Weekends were hectic, so I made no-fuss meals like yummy beef tips to bring us together at the end of the day.

—SUE GRONHOLZ BEAVER DAM, WI

PREP: 45 MIN. • **COOK:** 6 HOURS
MAKES: 8 SERVINGS

- 1 boneless beef chuck roast (about 2 pounds), cut into 2-inch pieces
- 1 teaspoon salt
- ¼ teaspoon pepper
- 2 tablespoons canola oil
- 1 medium onion, coarsely chopped
- 1 celery rib, coarsely chopped
- 6 garlic cloves, halved
- 2 cups beef broth
- 1½ cups dry red wine
- 1 fresh rosemary sprig
- 1 bay leaf
- 2 cans (4 ounces each) sliced mushrooms
- 2 tablespoons cornstarch
- ½ cup water
- 1 tablespoon balsamic vinegar
  Hot cooked egg noodles

1. Sprinkle the beef with salt and pepper. In a large skillet, heat oil over medium-high heat. Brown beef in batches. Remove with a slotted spoon to a 3- or 4-qt. slow cooker.
2. In the same pan, add onion and celery; cook and stir until tender, 6-8 minutes. Add garlic; cook 1 minute longer. Add broth, wine, rosemary and bay leaf. Bring to a boil; cook until liquid is reduced to about 2 cups, 8-10 minutes.
3. Pour over beef in slow cooker; stir in mushrooms. Cook, covered, on low until meat is tender, 6-8 hours. Remove rosemary and bay leaf.
4. In a small bowl, mix cornstarch, water and vinegar until smooth; gradually stir into beef mixture. Serve with noodles.

CHICKEN BISCUIT POTPIE

CHICKEN BISCUIT POTPIE

This meal-in-one takes just 10 minutes to assemble before popping it in the oven.

—DOROTHY SMITH EL DORADO, AR

PREP: 10 MIN. • **BAKE:** 25 MIN.
MAKES: 4 SERVINGS

- 1⅔ cups frozen mixed vegetables, thawed
- 1½ cups cubed cooked chicken
- 1 can (10¾ ounces) condensed cream of chicken soup, undiluted
- ¼ teaspoon dried thyme
- 1 cup biscuit/baking mix
- ½ cup milk
- 1 large egg

1. In a large bowl, combine the vegetables, chicken, soup and thyme. Pour into an ungreased deep-dish 9-in. pie plate. Combine the biscuit mix, milk and egg; spoon over the chicken mixture.
2. Bake at 400° until golden brown, 25-30 minutes.

GOES **GREAT** WITH

End the evening on a sweet note—bring out a plate full of Lemon Slice Sugar Cookies, page 88.

VEGETABLE & BEEF STUFFED RED PEPPERS

I love this recipe because it's one of the few ways I can get my husband to eat veggies! For a meatless version, replace the beef with eggplant and add more vegetables, like mushrooms or squash. You can also replace the rice with barley, couscous or even orzo.

—JENNIFER ZIMMERMAN AVONDALE, AZ

PREP: 35 MIN. • **BAKE:** 40 MIN.
MAKES: 6 SERVINGS

- 6 medium sweet red peppers
- 1 pound lean ground beef (90% lean)
- 1 tablespoon olive oil
- 1 medium zucchini, chopped
- 1 medium yellow summer squash, chopped
- 1 medium onion, finely chopped
- ⅓ cup finely chopped green pepper
- 2 cups coarsely chopped fresh spinach
- 4 garlic cloves, minced
- 1 cup ready-to-serve long grain and wild rice
- 1 can (8 ounces) tomato sauce
- ½ cup shredded part-skim mozzarella cheese
- ¼ teaspoon salt
- 3 slices reduced-fat provolone cheese, halved

1. Preheat oven to 350°. Cut and discard the tops from red peppers; remove seeds. In a 6-qt. stockpot, cook peppers in boiling water until crisp-tender, 3-5 minutes; drain and rinse in cold water.

2. In a large skillet, cook beef over medium heat 6-8 minutes or until no longer pink, breaking into crumbles. Remove with a slotted spoon; pour off drippings.

3. In the same pan, heat oil over medium heat; saute zucchini, yellow squash, onion and green pepper until tender, 4-5 minutes. Add the spinach and garlic; cook and stir until wilted, 1 minute. Stir in the cooked beef, rice, tomato sauce, mozzarella cheese and the salt.

4. Place the red peppers in a greased 8-in. square baking dish. Fill with meat mixture. Bake, covered, until peppers are tender, 35-40 minutes. Top with provolone cheese; bake, uncovered, until cheese is melted, 5 minutes.

GRANDMA'S CAJUN CHICKEN & SPAGHETTI

I'm originally from Louisiana, where my grandma spoke Cajun French as she taught me how to make her spicy chicken spaghetti on an old wood stove.

—BRENDA MELANCON MCCOMB, MS

PREP: 15 MIN. • **COOK:** 1¼ HOURS
MAKES: 10 SERVINGS

- 1 broiler/fryer chicken (3 to 4 pounds), cut up
- 1 to 1½ teaspoons cayenne pepper
- ¾ teaspoon salt
- 3 tablespoons canola oil
- 1 package (14 ounces) smoked sausage, sliced
- 1 large sweet onion, chopped
- 1 medium green pepper, chopped
- 1 celery rib, chopped
- 2 garlic cloves, minced
- 2 cans (14½ ounces each) diced tomatoes, undrained
- 1 can (14½ ounces) diced tomatoes with mild green chilies, undrained
- 1 package (16 ounces) spaghetti

1. Sprinkle chicken with cayenne and salt. In a Dutch oven, heat the oil over medium-high heat. Brown chicken in batches. Remove from pan.

2. Add sausage, onion, green pepper and celery to the same pan; cook and stir over medium heat 3 minutes. Add garlic; cook 1 minute longer. Stir in tomatoes. Return chicken to pan; bring to a boil. Reduce heat; simmer, covered, until chicken juices run clear, 1 hour.

3. Cook spaghetti according to package directions. Remove chicken from pan. When cool enough to handle, remove meat from bones; discard skin and bones. Shred meat with two forks; return to the pan. Bring to boil. Reduce heat; simmer, uncovered, until slightly thickened, 8-10 minutes. Skim fat. Drain the spaghetti; serve with chicken mixture.

VEGETABLE & BEEF STUFFED RED PEPPERS

EASY CHEESY
LOADED GRITS

Hearty Casseroles

Whether you want comfort food, a dish that's simple to pull together, or both, these one-pan dinners are too good to pass up. No matter the occasion, look no further than a tasty casserole.

EASY CHEESY LOADED GRITS

I was inspired to develop my own grits with sausage, green chilies and cheeses. The end result just might be better than the original.

—JOAN HALLFORD NORTH RICHLAND HILLS, TX

PREP: 35 MIN. • **BAKE:** 50 MIN. + STANDING
MAKES: 8 SERVINGS

- 1 pound mild or spicy bulk pork sausage
- 1 small onion, chopped
- 4 cups water
- ½ teaspoon salt
- 1 cup quick-cooking grits
- 3 cans (4 ounces each) chopped green chilies
- 1½ cups shredded sharp cheddar cheese, divided
- 1½ cups shredded Monterey Jack cheese, divided
- 2 tablespoons butter
- ¼ teaspoon hot pepper sauce
- 2 large eggs, lightly beaten
- ¼ teaspoon paprika
  Chopped fresh cilantro

1. Preheat oven to 325°. In a large skillet, cook sausage and onion over medium heat 6-8 minutes or until sausage is no longer pink, breaking up sausage into crumbles; drain.
2. In a large saucepan, bring water and salt to a boil. Slowly stir in grits. Reduce heat to medium-low; cook, covered, about 5 minutes or until thickened, stirring occasionally. Remove from heat.
3. Add the green chilies, ¾ cup cheddar cheese, ¾ cup Jack cheese, butter and pepper sauce; stir until cheese is melted. Stir in eggs, then sausage mixture.
4. Transfer to a greased 13x9-in. baking dish. Top with remaining cheeses; sprinkle with paprika. Bake, uncovered, until golden brown and set, 50-60 minutes. Let stand 10 minutes before serving. Sprinkle with cilantro.

HOT CHICKEN CASSEROLE

A comforting hot dish with a crisp top, this hearty casserole will warm you from the inside out.

—CAROL WILSON DEKALB, IL

PREP: 15 MIN. • **BAKE:** 40 MIN.
MAKES: 8 SERVINGS

- 3 cups cubed cooked chicken breast
- 2 cups mayonnaise
- 1 can (10¾ ounces) condensed cream of chicken soup, undiluted
- 2 celery ribs, finely chopped
- 2 cups cooked rice
- 1 can (8 ounces) sliced water chestnuts, drained
- 1 teaspoon grated onion
- 1 teaspoon lemon juice

TOPPING
- 2 cups crushed cornflakes
- ½ cup slivered almonds
- ½ cup butter, melted

1. Preheat oven to 350°. In a large bowl, combine the first eight ingredients. Transfer to a greased 13x9-in. baking dish.
2. Combine topping ingredients; sprinkle over top. Bake, uncovered, until bubbly, 40-45 minutes.
FREEZE OPTION *Cover and freeze unbaked casseroles up to 3 months. To use, remove from freezer 30 minutes before baking (do not thaw). Preheat the oven to 350°. Cover with foil and bake 1½ hours. Uncover; bake until bubbly and heated through, 10-15 minutes longer.*

TEST KITCHEN TIP
Wondering how much chicken to buy to make cubed cooked chicken? Generally, ¾ pound of boneless skinless chicken breasts will yield 2 cups of cubed cooked chicken. A 3½-pound whole chicken will yield about 3 cups.

CHILI BEEF CORN BREAD
CASSEROLE

CHILI BEEF CORN BREAD CASSEROLE

This recipe is my potluck standby. And when I hear that someone needs a good home-cooked meal, I bring this over.

—LORRAINE ESPENHAIN CORPUS CHRISTI, TX

PREP: 25 MIN. • **BAKE:** 25 MIN.
MAKES: 6 SERVINGS

- 1 **pound ground beef**
- 1 **tablespoon cornstarch**
- 1 **tablespoon dried minced onion**
- 1 **teaspoon chili powder**
- ½ **teaspoon garlic powder**
- 1 **can (15 ounces) tomato sauce**
- ¾ **cup all-purpose flour**
- ¾ **cup yellow cornmeal**
- 3 **tablespoons sugar**
- 2 **teaspoons baking powder**
- 2 **large eggs**
- ½ **cup 2% milk**
- 3 **tablespoons canola oil**
- 1 **can (8¾ ounces) cream-style corn**
- 1 **cup shredded cheddar cheese**
  Sour cream and salsa, optional

1. Preheat oven to 375°. In a large skillet, cook beef over medium heat 6-8 minutes or until no longer pink, breaking into crumbles; drain. Stir in cornstarch, onion, chili powder and garlic powder. Stir in tomato sauce. Cook and stir 2 minutes or until thickened. Remove from heat.
2. In a large bowl, whisk the flour, cornmeal, sugar and baking powder. In another bowl, whisk eggs, milk and oil until blended; stir in corn. Add to the flour mixture; stir just until moistened. Stir in cheese.
3. Spread half of the batter into a greased 2-qt. baking dish. Top with beef mixture. Spread remaining batter over filling.
4. Bake, uncovered, until a toothpick inserted in corn bread portion comes out clean, 25-30 minutes. Let stand 5 minutes before serving. If desired, serve with sour cream and salsa.

HAM & VEGGIE CASSEROLE

FAST FIX
HAM & VEGGIE CASSEROLE

I've paired ham with broccoli and cauliflower for years. To complete this casserole dinner, I simply pass around the dinner rolls.

—SHERRI MELOTIK OAK CREEK, WI

START TO FINISH: 30 MIN.
MAKES: 4 SERVINGS

- 1 **package (16 ounces) frozen broccoli florets**
- 1 **package (16 ounces) frozen cauliflower**
- 2 **teaspoons plus 2 tablespoons butter, divided**
- ¼ **cup seasoned bread crumbs**
- 2 **tablespoons all-purpose flour**
- 1½ **cups 2% milk**
- ¾ **cup shredded sharp cheddar cheese**
- ½ **cup grated Parmesan cheese**
- 1½ **cups cubed fully cooked ham (about 8 ounces)**
- ¼ **teaspoon pepper**

1. Preheat oven to 425°. Cook broccoli and cauliflower according to package directions; drain.
2. Meanwhile, in a small skillet, melt 2 teaspoons butter. Add bread crumbs; cook and stir over medium heat 2-3 minutes or until lightly toasted. Remove from heat.
3. In a large saucepan, melt the remaining butter over medium heat. Stir in flour until smooth; gradually whisk in milk. Bring to a boil, stirring constantly; cook and stir 1-2 minutes or until thickened. Remove from heat; stir in cheeses until blended. Stir in ham, pepper and vegetables.
4. Transfer to a greased 8-in. square baking dish. Sprinkle with toasted crumbs. Bake, uncovered, until heated through, 10-15 minutes.

GOES GREAT WITH

A casserole this delicious deserves a great dessert, such as a plate full of warm homemade cookies.

CHICKEN CORDON BLEU BAKE

A friend shared this awesome hot dish recipe with me. I freeze several pans to share with neighbors or for days when I'm scrambling at mealtime.
—**REA NEWELL** DECATUR, IL

PREP: 20 MIN. • **BAKE:** 40 MIN.
MAKES: 2 CASSEROLES (6 SERVINGS EACH)

- 2 packages (6 ounces each) reduced-sodium stuffing mix
- 1 can (10¾ ounces) condensed cream of chicken soup, undiluted
- 1 cup 2% milk
- 8 cups cubed cooked chicken
- ½ teaspoon pepper
- ¾ pound sliced deli ham, cut into 1-inch strips
- 1 cup shredded Swiss cheese
- 3 cups shredded cheddar cheese

1. Preheat oven to 350°. Prepare stuffing mixes according to package directions. Meanwhile, whisk together soup and milk.
2. Toss chicken with pepper; divide between two greased 13x9-in. baking dishes. Layer with ham, Swiss cheese, 1 cup cheddar cheese, soup mixture and stuffing. Sprinkle with remaining cheddar cheese.
3. Bake, covered, 30 minutes. Uncover; bake until the cheese is melted, 10-15 minutes.
FREEZE OPTION *Cover and freeze unbaked casseroles. To use, partially thaw in the refrigerator overnight. Remove from refrigerator 30 minutes before baking. Preheat oven to 350°. Bake, covered, until heated through and a thermometer inserted in the center reads 165°, about 45 minutes. Uncover; bake until cheese is melted, 10-15 minutes.*

TEST KITCHEN TIP
Add another flavor layer (and crunch!) to this recipe by sprinkling crumbled cooked bacon on top.

CHICKEN CORDON BLEU BAKE

NEW ENGLAND BEAN & BOG CASSOULET
Devon Delaney
Westport, CT

TURKEY ALFREDO TETRAZZINI

I speed up my mother-in-law's tetrazzini recipe by using jarred Alfredo sauce, canned mushrooms and onion powder. We love the peas' pop of color, the hint of white wine and the creamy, tangy taste.
—JUDY BATSON TAMPA, FL

PREP: 20 MIN. • **BAKE:** 30 MIN.
MAKES: 4 SERVINGS

- 4 ounces thin spaghetti
- 1 jar (15 ounces) Alfredo sauce
- 2 cups frozen peas
- 1½ cups cubed cooked turkey or chicken
- 1 can (4 ounces) mushroom stems and pieces, drained
- ¼ cup shredded Swiss cheese
- ¼ cup shredded Parmesan cheese
- 2 tablespoons white wine or chicken broth
- ½ teaspoon onion powder
- ½ cup french-fried onions
- ½ teaspoon paprika

1. Cook spaghetti according to package directions. Meanwhile, in a large bowl, combine Alfredo sauce, peas, turkey, mushrooms, cheeses, wine and onion powder. Drain spaghetti. Add to sauce mixture; toss to coat. Transfer to a greased 8-in. square baking dish. Sprinkle with onions and paprika.
2. Cover and bake at 350° until heated through, 30-35 minutes.

★ ★ ★ ★ ★ **READER REVIEW**
"Very good. I will make this dish again but will try reducing the amount of peas and adding some water chestnuts, celery and garlic."
JORG TASTEOFHOME.COM

NEW ENGLAND BEAN & BOG CASSOULET

When I moved to New England, I fully embraced the local cuisine. My cassoulet with baked beans pays tribute to a French classic and to New England.
—**DEVON DELANEY** WESTPORT, CT

PREP: 15 MIN. • **COOK:** 35 MIN.
MAKES: 8 SERVINGS (3½ QUARTS)

- 5 tablespoons olive oil, divided
- 8 boneless skinless chicken thighs (about 2 pounds)
- 1 package (12 ounces) fully cooked Italian chicken sausage links, cut into ½-inch slices
- 4 shallots, finely chopped
- 2 teaspoons minced fresh rosemary or ½ teaspoon dried rosemary, crushed
- 2 teaspoons minced fresh thyme or ½ teaspoon dried thyme
- 1 can (28 ounces) fire-roasted diced tomatoes, undrained
- 1 can (16 ounces) baked beans
- 1 cup chicken broth
- ½ cup fresh or frozen cranberries
- 3 day-old croissants, cubed (about 6 cups)
- ½ teaspoon lemon-pepper seasoning
- 2 tablespoons minced fresh parsley

1. Preheat oven to 400°. In a Dutch oven, heat 2 tablespoons oil over medium heat. In batches, brown chicken thighs on both sides; remove from pan, reserving drippings. Add sausage; cook and stir until lightly browned. Remove from pan.
2. In the same pan, heat 1 tablespoon oil over medium heat. Add shallots, rosemary and thyme; cook and stir until shallots are tender, 1-2 minutes. Stir in tomatoes, beans, broth and cranberries. Return chicken and sausage to pan; bring to a boil. Bake, covered, until the chicken is tender, 20-25 minutes.
3. Toss the croissant pieces with remaining oil; sprinkle with the lemon pepper. Arrange over the chicken mixture. Bake, uncovered, until croissants are golden brown, 12-15 minutes. Sprinkle with parsley.

MINI REUBEN CASSEROLES

ALMOND TURKEY CASSEROLE

One of my cousins shared the recipe for this comforting casserole. The almonds and water chestnuts give it a fun crunch.

—**JILL BLACK** TROY, ON

PREP: 10 MIN. • **BAKE:** 35 MIN.
MAKES: 8 SERVINGS

2 cans (10¾ ounces each) condensed cream of mushroom soup, undiluted
½ cup mayonnaise
½ cup sour cream
2 tablespoons chopped onion
2 tablespoons lemon juice
1 teaspoon salt
½ teaspoon white pepper
5 cups cubed cooked turkey
3 cups cooked rice
4 celery ribs, chopped
1 can (8 ounces) sliced water chestnuts, drained
1 cup sliced almonds

TOPPING

1½ cups crushed Ritz crackers (about 40 crackers)
⅓ cup butter, melted
¼ cup sliced almonds

1. In a large bowl, combine soup, mayonnaise, sour cream, onion, lemon juice, salt and pepper. Stir in turkey, rice, celery, water chestnuts and almonds.
2. Transfer to a greased 13x9-in. baking dish. Bake, uncovered, at 350° for 25 minutes. Combine topping ingredients; sprinkle over turkey mixture. Return to oven; bake until bubbly and golden brown, another 10-15 minutes.

★ ★ ★ ★ ★ **READER REVIEW**

"Very tasty. My kids even went back for seconds. Leftovers tasted just as good the next day for lunch, too."

MAYBAKE TASTEOFHOME.COM

MINI REUBEN CASSEROLES

These cute and creamy individual roast beef casseroles have all the classic flavors of a Reuben sandwich, presented in a brand-new format.

—*TASTE OF HOME* TEST KITCHEN

PREP: 20 MIN. • **BAKE:** 20 MIN.
MAKES: 4 SERVINGS

1 medium onion, chopped
1 medium green pepper, chopped
2 teaspoons olive oil
2 cups cubed cooked beef roast
1 can (14 ounces) sauerkraut, rinsed and well drained
1 can (10¾ ounces) condensed cream of chicken soup, undiluted
1¼ cups shredded Swiss cheese, divided
⅓ cup 2% milk
½ cup Thousand Island salad dressing
2 slices rye bread, cubed
1 tablespoon butter, melted
½ teaspoon onion powder

1. Preheat oven to 350°. In a large skillet, saute onion and pepper in oil until tender. Stir in beef, sauerkraut, soup, 1 cup cheese, milk and salad dressing; heat through. Transfer to four greased 10-oz. ramekins or custard cups. Place ramekins on a baking sheet.
2. In a small bowl, toss the bread cubes with butter and onion powder. Arrange over tops. Bake, uncovered, 15 minutes. Sprinkle with remaining cheese. Bake until cheese is melted, 5-10 minutes longer.

**ALMOND TURKEY
CASSEROLE**

FOURTH OF JULY BEAN CASSEROLE

FOURTH OF JULY BEAN CASSEROLE

The outstanding barbecue taste of these beans makes them a favorite for meals all summer and into the fall. It's a popular dish with everyone, even kids. Having meat in with the beans is so much better than plain pork and beans.

—DONNA FANCHER LAWRENCE, IN

PREP: 20 MIN. • **BAKE:** 1 HOUR
MAKES: 12 SERVINGS

- ½ pound bacon strips, diced
- ½ pound ground beef
- 1 cup chopped onion
- 1 can (28 ounces) pork and beans
- 1 can (16 ounces) kidney beans, rinsed and drained
- 1 can (15¼ ounces) lima beans
- ½ cup barbecue sauce
- ½ cup ketchup
- ½ cup sugar
- ½ cup packed brown sugar
- 2 tablespoons prepared mustard
- 2 tablespoons molasses
- 1 teaspoon salt
- ½ teaspoon chili powder

1. In a large skillet, cook bacon, beef and onion until meat is no longer pink; drain.
2. Transfer to a greased 2½-qt. baking dish; add all of the beans and mix well. In a small bowl, combine the remaining ingredients; stir into beef and bean mixture.
3. Cover and bake at 350° for 45 minutes. Uncover; bake 15 minutes longer.

★ ★ ★ ★ ★ **READER REVIEW**

"I have to say this is the best bean recipe ever. I make it for both our summer cookouts and Christmas dinner. It goes great with ham. Everyone loves it and looks forward to it."

NENE1 TASTEOFHOME.COM

HEARTY BEEF CASSEROLE

Your little ones who refuse to eat veggies won't complain one bit when you bring this cheesy casserole with a corn bread crust to the table. You can always cut back on the Cajun seasoning if necessary.

—**KELLY CIEPLUCH** KENOSHA, WI

PREP: 15 MIN. • **BAKE:** 25 MIN.
MAKES: 6 SERVINGS

- 1 package (8½ ounces) corn bread/muffin mix
- 1 pound ground beef
- 2 cans (14½ ounces each) diced tomatoes, drained
- 2 cups frozen mixed vegetables, thawed
- 1 can (6 ounces) tomato paste
- 1 to 2 teaspoons Cajun seasoning
- 1 cup (4 ounces) shredded cheddar cheese
- 2 green onions, thinly sliced

1. Preheat oven to 350°. Prepare corn bread batter according to package directions. Spread into a greased 11x7-in. baking dish.
2. In a large skillet, cook beef over medium heat until no longer pink; drain. Add tomatoes, vegetables, tomato paste and seasoning. Bring to a boil. Reduce the heat; simmer, uncovered, for 5 minutes. Pour over batter. Sprinkle with cheese.
3. Bake, uncovered, until golden brown, 25-30 minutes. Sprinkle with green onions.

FREEZE OPTION *Omit onion topping. Cool baked casserole; wrap and freeze. To use, partially thaw in the refrigerator overnight. Remove 30 minutes before baking. Preheat oven to 350°; bake as directed, increasing time as necessary for a thermometer inserted in center to read 165°. Sprinkle cooked casserole with onions.*

BAKED ORANGE ROUGHY & RICE

It might sound too good to be true, but this delectable fish dinner requires only one dish. Your family will be lining up to dig in once they see the beautiful results!

—*TASTE OF HOME* TEST KITCHEN

PREP: 10 MIN. • **BAKE:** 30 MIN.
MAKES: 4 SERVINGS

- 2 cups uncooked instant rice
- 1 package (16 ounces) frozen broccoli-cauliflower blend, thawed
- 4 orange roughy fillets (6 ounces each)
- 1 can (14½ ounces) chicken broth
- 1 can (14½ ounces) fire-roasted diced tomatoes, undrained
- 1 teaspoon garlic powder
- 1 teaspoon lemon-pepper seasoning
- ¼ to ½ teaspoon cayenne pepper
- ½ cup shredded cheddar cheese

1. Place rice in a greased 13x9-in. baking dish. Layer with the vegetables and fish. Pour the broth and tomatoes over the top; sprinkle with seasonings.
2. Cover and bake at 375° until fish flakes easily with a fork and rice is tender, 25-30 minutes. Sprinkle with cheese; bake until cheese is melted, 5 minutes longer.

GOES GREAT WITH

What does this casserole need? A slice or two of Megumi Garcia's Crusty Homemade Bread, page 69, on the side!

HEARTY BEEF CASSEROLE

BAKED CHOPS & FRIES

BAKED CHOPS & FRIES

Convenience items such as frozen vegetables and a jar of cheese sauce make it a snap to assemble this pork chop supper. It's a simple one-dish meal.

—**GREGG VOSS** EMERSON, NE

PREP: 20 MIN. • **BAKE:** 55 MIN.
MAKES: 6 SERVINGS

- 6 bone-in pork loin chops (1 inch thick and 7 ounces each)
- 1 tablespoon olive oil
- ½ teaspoon seasoned salt
- 1 jar (8 ounces) process cheese sauce
- ½ cup 2% milk
- 4 cups frozen cottage fries
- 1 can (2.8 ounces) french-fried onions, divided
- 4 cups frozen broccoli florets

1. In a large skillet, brown pork chops in oil; sprinkle with seasoned salt. In a small bowl, combine cheese sauce and milk until blended.
2. Spread into a greased 13x9-in. baking dish. Top with cottage fries and half of the onions. Layer with broccoli and pork chops.
3. Cover and bake at 350° for 45 minutes. Sprinkle with remaining onions. Bake 10 minutes longer or until a thermometer reads 160°.

PUFF PASTRY CHICKEN POTPIE

When my wife is craving comfort food, I whip up my chicken potpie. It's easy to make, sticks to your ribs and delivers soul-satisfying flavor.

—**NICK IVERSON** MILWAUKEE, WI

PREP: 45 MIN. • **BAKE:** 45 MIN. + STANDING
MAKES: 8 SERVINGS

- 1 package (17.3 ounces) frozen puff pastry, thawed
- 2 pounds boneless skinless chicken breasts, cut into 1-inch pieces
- 1 teaspoon salt, divided
- 1 teaspoon pepper, divided
- 4 tablespoons butter, divided
- 1 large onion, chopped
- 2 garlic cloves, minced
- 1 teaspoon minced fresh thyme or ¼ teaspoon dried thyme
- 1 teaspoon minced fresh sage or ¼ teaspoon rubbed sage

PUFF PASTRY CHICKEN POTPIE

- ½ cup all-purpose flour
- 2 cups chicken broth
- 1 cup plus 1 tablespoon half-and-half cream, divided
- 2 cups frozen mixed vegetables (about 10 ounces)
- 1 tablespoon lemon juice
- 1 large egg yolk

1. Preheat oven to 400°. On a lightly floured surface, roll each pastry sheet into a 12x10-in. rectangle. Cut one sheet crosswise into six 2-in. strips; cut remaining sheet lengthwise into five 2-in. strips. On a baking sheet, closely weave strips to make a 12x10-in. lattice. Freeze while making the filling.
2. Toss chicken with ½ teaspoon each salt and pepper. In a large skillet, heat 1 tablespoon butter over medium-high heat; saute chicken

until browned, 5-7 minutes. Remove from pan.
3. In the same skillet, heat remaining butter over medium-high heat; saute onion until tender, 5-7 minutes. Stir in the garlic and herbs; cook 1 minute. Stir in flour until blended; cook and stir 1 minute. Gradually stir in broth and 1 cup cream. Bring to a boil, stirring constantly; cook and stir until thickened, about 2 minutes.
4. Stir in vegetables, lemon juice, chicken and the remaining salt and pepper; return to a boil. Transfer to a greased 2-qt. oblong baking dish. Top with lattice, trimming to fit.
5. Whisk together egg yolk and remaining cream; brush over pastry. Bake, uncovered, until bubbly and golden brown, 45-55 minutes. Let stand 15 minutes before serving.

CHICKEN
TAMALE BAKE
Jennifer Stowell
Montezuma, IA

CHICKEN TAMALE BAKE

When I serve this Mexican-style casserole, everyone ends up with a clean plate award. Offer fresh toppings like green onions, tomatoes and avocado.

—JENNIFER STOWELL MONTEZUMA, IA

PREP: 10 MIN. • **BAKE:** 25 MIN. + STANDING
MAKES: 8 SERVINGS

- 1 **large egg, lightly beaten**
- 1 **can (14¾ ounces) cream-style corn**
- 1 **package (8½ ounces) corn bread/muffin mix**
- 1 **can (4 ounces) chopped green chilies**
- ⅓ **cup 2% milk**
- ¼ **cup shredded Mexican cheese blend**

TOPPING
- 2 **cups coarsely shredded cooked chicken**
- 1 **can (10 ounces) enchilada sauce**
- 1 **teaspoon ground cumin**
- ½ **teaspoon onion powder**
- 1¾ **cups shredded Mexican cheese blend**
  Chopped green onions, tomatoes and avocado, optional

1. Preheat oven to 400°. In a large bowl, combine first six ingredients; stir just until dry ingredients are moistened. Transfer to a greased 13x9-in. baking dish. Bake until light golden brown and a toothpick inserted in center comes out clean, 15-18 minutes.

2. In a large skillet, combine chicken, enchilada sauce, cumin and onion powder; bring to a boil, stirring occasionally. Reduce heat; simmer, uncovered, 5 minutes. Spread over corn bread layer; sprinkle with cheese.

3. Bake until cheese is melted, 10-12 minutes longer. Let stand 10 minutes before serving. If desired, top with green onions, tomatoes and avocado.

TEST KITCHEN TIP
Here's a quick, fuss-free way to get rid of an avocado pit: Slip a tablespoon under the seed to loosen it from the fruit. Easy peasy!

BAKED SIMPLE MEATBALL STROGANOFF

If you like meatball subs, you'll love this tangy casserole that has all the rich taste of the popular sandwiches...with none of the mess. The Italian bread is spread with a cream cheese mixture, then topped with meatballs, spaghetti sauce and cheese. Bravo!

—GINA HARRIS SENECA, SC

PREP: 40 MIN. • **BAKE:** 30 MIN.
MAKES: 6 SERVINGS

- ⅓ cup chopped green onions
- ¼ cup seasoned bread crumbs
- 3 tablespoons grated Parmesan cheese
- 1 pound ground beef
- 1 loaf (1 pound) Italian bread, cut into 1-inch slices
- 1 package (8 ounces) cream cheese, softened
- ½ cup mayonnaise
- 1 teaspoon Italian seasoning
- ¼ teaspoon pepper
- 2 cups shredded part-skim mozzarella cheese
- 3½ cups spaghetti sauce
- 1 cup water
- 2 garlic cloves, minced

1. In a large bowl, combine the onions, bread crumbs and Parmesan cheese. Crumble beef over mixture and mix well. Shape into 1-in. balls; place on a greased rack in a shallow baking pan. Bake at 400° until no longer pink, 15-20 minutes.

2. Meanwhile, arrange bread in a single layer in an ungreased 13x9-in. baking dish (all of the bread might not be used). Combine the cream cheese, mayonnaise, Italian seasoning and pepper; spread over the bread. Sprinkle with ½ cup mozzarella.

3. Combine the spaghetti sauce, water and garlic; add meatballs. Pour over cheese mixture; sprinkle with the remaining mozzarella. Bake, uncovered, at 350° until heated through, 30 minutes.

BAKED SIMPLE MEATBALL STROGANOFF

EGGPLANT & ZUCCHINI ROLLATINI

EGGPLANT & ZUCCHINI ROLLATINI

Someone at the table is bound to praise your rollatini dish, then ask what it actually is! Your answer: thin slices of eggplant that are lightly breaded and fried, covered with cheeses, rolled up, topped with tangy tomato sauce and baked.

—**ANDREA RIVERA** WESTBURY, NY

PREP: 1 HOUR + STANDING • **BAKE:** 30 MIN.
MAKES: 8 SERVINGS

- 1 **large eggplant**
- ½ **teaspoon salt**

SAUCE
- ⅓ **cup chopped onion**
- 3 **garlic cloves, minced**
- 1 **tablespoon olive oil**
- 2 **cans (28 ounces each) crushed tomatoes**
- ¼ **cup dry red wine or vegetable broth**
- 1 **tablespoon sugar**
- 2 **teaspoons each dried oregano and dried basil**
- 1 **teaspoon salt**
- ¼ **teaspoon pepper**

ROLLATINI
- 4 **cups shredded part-skim mozzarella cheese**
- 1 **package (8 ounces) cream cheese, softened and cubed**
- 1 **large zucchini, thinly sliced**
- 2 **tablespoons plus ½ cup olive oil, divided**
- 2 **large eggs, lightly beaten**
- 1 **cup dry bread crumbs**
- ½ **cup grated Parmesan cheese**

1. Peel and slice eggplant lengthwise into sixteen ⅛-in.-thick slices. Place in a colander over a plate; sprinkle with salt and toss. Let stand for 30 minutes. Rinse and drain.

2. In a large saucepan, saute onion and garlic in oil until tender. Add the remaining sauce ingredients. Bring to a boil. Reduce the heat; simmer, uncovered, for 20-25 minutes to allow flavors to blend, stirring occasionally.

3. Preheat oven to 350°. In a large bowl, combine mozzarella and cream cheese; mix well. In a large skillet, saute zucchini in 2 tablespoons oil until tender; remove and set aside.

4. Place eggs and bread crumbs in separate shallow bowls. Dip eggplant in eggs, then bread crumbs. Fry eggplant in remaining oil in batches for 2-3 minutes on each side or until golden brown. Drain on paper towels.

5. Spoon 1 cup of the sauce into an ungreased 13x9-in. baking dish. Layer eggplant slices with zucchini; top each with 3 tablespoons cheese mixture. Roll up and place seam side down in baking dish. Top with remaining sauce. Cover and bake until bubbly, 30-35 minutes. Sprinkle with the Parmesan cheese.

SEAFOOD CASSEROLE

A family favorite, this rice casserole is stuffed with plenty of seafood and veggies. It's hearty, homey and so easy to make!

—**NANCY BILLUPS** PRINCETON, IA

PREP: 20 MIN. • **BAKE:** 40 MIN.
MAKES: 6 SERVINGS

- 1 **package (6 ounces) long grain and wild rice**
- 1 **pound frozen crabmeat, thawed or 2½ cups canned lump crabmeat, drained**
- 1 **pound cooked medium shrimp, peeled, deveined and cut into ½-inch pieces**
- 2 **celery ribs, chopped**
- 1 **medium onion, finely chopped**
- ½ **cup finely chopped green pepper**
- 1 **can (4 ounces) mushroom stems and pieces, drained**
- 1 **jar (2 ounces) diced pimientos, drained**
- 1 **cup mayonnaise**
- 1 **cup 2% milk**
- ½ **teaspoon pepper**
  Dash Worcestershire sauce
- ¼ **cup dry bread crumbs**

1. Cook rice according to package directions. Meanwhile, preheat oven to 375°.

2. In a large bowl, combine crab, shrimp, celery, onion, green pepper, mushrooms and pimientos. In a small bowl, whisk mayonnaise, milk, pepper and Worcestershire sauce; stir into seafood mixture. Stir in rice.

3. Transfer to a greased 13x9-in. baking dish. Sprinkle with bread crumbs. Bake, uncovered, until bubbly, 40-50 minutes.

JUICY
WATERMELON
SALAD

Salads

Whether the ingredients come from the grocery store, farmers market or your own garden, let these fresh, flavorful, colorful salads shine at your next meal.

JUICY WATERMELON SALAD

This salad has such an unexpected mix of flavors that friends often ask for the recipe. Combine red, pink and yellow seedless watermelon for a colorful twist.
—**HEIDI HAIGHT** MACOMB, MI

PREP: 20 MIN. + CHILLING
MAKES: 10 SERVINGS

- 8 **cups cubed seedless watermelon (about 1 medium)**
- 1 **small red onion, cut into rings**
- 1 **cup coarsely chopped macadamia nuts or slivered almonds, toasted**
- 1 **cup fresh arugula or baby spinach**
- ⅓ **cup balsamic vinaigrette**
- 3 **tablespoons canola oil**
  Watermelon slices, optional
- 1 **cup (4 ounces) crumbled blue cheese**

In a large bowl, combine watermelon and onion; cover and refrigerate until cold, about 30 minutes. Just before serving, add macadamia nuts and arugula to watermelon mixture. In a small bowl, whisk vinaigrette and oil; drizzle over the salad and toss to coat. If desired, serve salad over the sliced watermelon. Sprinkle with cheese.
NOTE *To toast nuts, bake in a shallow pan in a 350° oven for 5-10 minutes or cook in a skillet over low heat until lightly browned, stirring occasionally.*

★ ★ ★ ★ ★ **READER REVIEW**
"It's surprising to put the cheese and onions with watermelon, but so good! I served as a side at a party; was a big hit!"
MRSDUMAIS TASTEOFHOME.COM

MY UNDERGROUND VEGETABLE SALAD

I have found that roasting is a delicious way to get bring out the subtle sweetness of rich, earthy root vegetables. Serving them over fresh endive with a homemade vinaigrette is just a bonus!
—**PETER HALFERTY** CORPUS CHRISTI, TX

PREP: 20 MIN. • **BAKE:** 40 MIN.
MAKES: 8 SERVINGS

- 1 **pound medium fresh mushrooms, halved**
- 8 **small carrots, peeled and halved lengthwise**
- 2 **cups cubed peeled celery root (about ½ pound)**
- 2 **cups cubed peeled rutabaga (about 1 medium)**
- 2 **cups cubed peeled sweet potatoes (about 1 medium)**
- 2 **tablespoons olive oil**
- ¼ **teaspoon salt**
- 2 **cups cherry tomatoes, halved**
- 8 **cups torn curly endive**

VINAIGRETTE

- 3 **tablespoons apple cider or juice**
- 2 **tablespoons lemon juice**
- 2 **tablespoons cider vinegar**
- 1 **teaspoon stone-ground mustard**
- 1 **teaspoon grated lemon peel**
- ½ **teaspoon fennel seed, crushed**
- ¼ **teaspoon salt**
- ¼ **teaspoon pepper**
- ½ **cup olive oil**

1. Preheat oven to 400°. In a large bowl, combine first five ingredients. Add oil and salt; toss to coat. Transfer to a greased shallow roasting pan. Roast for 30-35 minutes or until the vegetables are tender, stirring them occasionally. Add the tomatoes; bake 10 minutes longer.
2. Place endive in a large bowl. In a small bowl, whisk the first eight vinaigrette ingredients. Gradually whisk in the oil until blended. Pour over the endive; toss to coat. Divide endive among eight plates; top with roasted vegetables.

(5) INGREDIENTS **FAST FIX** ▶
JEWELED ENDIVE SALAD

My friends have a huge potluck party during the holidays. I wanted to bring something unique, so I topped off endive and watercress with pretty, jewel-toned pomegranate seeds.

—ALYSHA BRAUN ST. CATHARINES, ON

START TO FINISH: 15 MIN.
MAKES: 8 SERVINGS

- 1 **bunch watercress (4 ounces)**
- 2 **heads endive, halved lengthwise and thinly sliced**
- 1 **cup pomegranate seeds (about 1 pomegranate)**
- 1 **shallot, thinly sliced**

DRESSING
- ⅓ **cup olive oil**
- 3 **tablespoons lemon juice**
- 2 **teaspoons grated lemon peel**
- ¼ **teaspoon salt**
- ⅛ **teaspoon pepper**

1. In a large bowl, combine the watercress, endive, pomegranate seeds and shallot.
2. In a small bowl, whisk the dressing ingredients. Drizzle over salad; toss to coat.

(5) INGREDIENTS **FAST FIX** ▶
INSALATA CAPRESE

A classic caprese salad makes you think you're in Italy. For extra zing, I add a splash of balsamic vinegar.

—JOE COLAMONICO NORTH CHARLESTON, SC

START TO FINISH: 25 MIN.
MAKES: 8 SERVINGS

- 2½ **pounds plum tomatoes (about 10), cut into 1-inch pieces**
- 1 **carton (8 ounces) fresh mozzarella cheese pearls**
- ½ **cup pitted ripe olives**
- 3 **tablespoons olive oil**
- ¼ **cup thinly sliced fresh basil**
- 2 **teaspoons minced fresh oregano**
- ½ **teaspoon salt**
- ¼ **teaspoon pepper**
  Balsamic vinegar, optional

In a large bowl, mix tomatoes, cheese pearls and olives. Drizzle with oil. Sprinkle with basil, oregano, salt and pepper; toss to coat. Let stand 10 minutes before serving. If desired, drizzle with vinegar.

★ ★ ★ ★ ★ **READER REVIEW**
"Just perfect! I used cherry tomatoes and cut them in half. I did add the balsamic vinegar, and it was so good with the fresh herbs."

DEBORALZ TASTEOFHOME.COM

YOU'RE-BACON-ME-CRAZY POTATO SALAD

The stuff from the deli just isn't our thing, but for us it isn't a summer cookout without potato salad. I tried out many recipes until I developed this one. Now if I even mention grilling or barbecuing, this side dish is my family's top request.
—PAUL COGSWELL LEAGUE CITY, TX

PREP: 10 MIN. • **COOK:** 25 MIN. + CHILLING
MAKES: 12 SERVINGS (¾ CUP EACH)

- 2½ pounds small red potatoes, cut into 1-inch pieces
- 3 teaspoons salt
- 1 pound bacon strips, finely chopped
- 1 large onion, chopped
- 3 celery ribs, finely chopped
- 2 cups mayonnaise
- 2 tablespoons Dijon or yellow mustard
- ¾ teaspoon dill weed
- ½ teaspoon celery salt
- ¼ teaspoon celery seed

1. Place potatoes in a 6-qt. stockpot; add water to cover. Add salt; bring to a boil. Reduce heat; cook, uncovered, 12-15 minutes or until the potatoes are tender.
2. Meanwhile, in a large skillet, cook bacon over medium heat until crisp, stirring occasionally. Remove with a slotted spoon and drain bacon on paper towels; reserve 4 tablespoons bacon drippings. Cook and stir onion in reserved drippings 6-8 minutes or until browned.
3. Reserve ¼ cup cooked bacon for topping. Add onion, drippings, celery and remaining bacon to potatoes.
4. In a small bowl, mix mayonnaise, mustard and seasonings. Pour over the potato mixture; toss to coat. Refrigerate, covered, 1 hour or until chilled. Just before serving, sprinkle with reserved bacon.

YOU'RE-BACON-ME-CRAZY POTATO SALAD

AVOCADO & CHICKPEA QUINOA SALAD

This delicious salad is high in protein and holds well in the fridge for a few days. If you make it ahead, add the avocados and tomatoes right before serving.
—ELIZABETH BENNETT SEATTLE, WA

PREP: 25 MIN. • **COOK:** 15 MIN.
MAKES: 6 SERVINGS

- 1 cup quinoa, rinsed
- 1 can (15 ounces) chickpeas, rinsed and drained
- 2 cups cherry tomatoes, halved
- 1 cup (4 ounces) crumbled feta cheese
- ½ medium ripe avocado, peeled and cubed
- 4 green onions, chopped (about ½ cup)

DRESSING
- 3 tablespoons white wine vinegar
- 1 teaspoon Dijon mustard
- ¼ teaspoon kosher salt
- ¼ teaspoon garlic powder
- ¼ teaspoon freshly ground pepper
- ¼ cup olive oil

1. Cook quinoa according to package directions; transfer to a large bowl and cool slightly.
2. Add chickpeas, tomatoes, cheese, avocado and green onions to quinoa; gently stir to combine. In a small bowl, whisk first five dressing ingredients. Gradually whisk in oil until blended. Drizzle over the salad; gently toss to coat. Refrigerate leftovers.
NOTE *Look for quinoa in the cereal, rice or organic food aisle.*

✱
TEST KITCHEN TIP
Want to give this salad a different taste and texture? You can keep the fiber when you exchange quinoa for brown rice or barley.

FRESH BROCCOLI
SALAD WITH LEMON

FRESH BROCCOLI SALAD WITH LEMON

This salad has a hint of sweetness in the dressing, which contrasts with the indulgent bacon. Swap cauliflower for the broccoli if you prefer.
—JANET ROTH TEMPE, AZ

START TO FINISH: 30 MIN.
MAKES: 12 SERVINGS (1 CUP EACH)

- ¼ cup cider vinegar
- ¼ cup lemon juice
- ½ cup reduced-fat mayonnaise
- ¼ cup sugar
- 2 tablespoons prepared mustard
- 1 teaspoon garlic salt
- ⅛ teaspoon pepper
- 6 ounces cream cheese, softened
- 14 cups small broccoli florets (about 2¼ pounds)
- 12 ounces fresh mushrooms, stems removed, chopped
- 16 bacon strips, cooked and crumbled
- 1 cup raisins
- ⅓ cup chopped red onion
  Lemon wedges, optional

1. Place the first eight ingredients in a blender; cover blender and process until smooth.
2. In a large bowl, combine broccoli, mushrooms, bacon, raisins and onion. Pour dressing over salad; toss to coat. Refrigerate until serving. If desired, serve with lemon wedges.

For a complete, elegant meal, pair this salad with Tracy Tylkowski's Balsamic Roast Chicken on page 7—and add some dinner rolls on the side!

RED & GREEN SALAD WITH TOASTED ALMONDS
Jasmine Rose
Crystal Lake, IL

RED & GREEN SALAD WITH TOASTED ALMONDS

During a long Midwest winter, I crave greens and tomatoes from the garden. This salad has a fantastic out-of-the-garden taste. Thank goodness I can get the ingredients all year-round!
—JASMINE ROSE CRYSTAL LAKE, IL

START TO FINISH: 25 MIN.
MAKES: 12 SERVINGS (1⅓ CUPS EACH)

- ¼ cup red wine vinegar
- 1 tablespoon reduced-sodium soy sauce
- 2 garlic cloves, minced
- 2 teaspoons sesame oil
- 2 teaspoons honey
- 1 teaspoon minced fresh gingerroot or ½ teaspoon ground ginger
- ⅛ teaspoon Louisiana-style hot sauce
- ½ cup grapeseed or canola oil

SALAD
- 2 heads Boston or Bibb lettuce, torn
- 1 head red leaf lettuce
- 1 medium sweet red pepper, julienned
- 2 celery ribs, sliced
- 1 cup sliced English cucumber
- 1 cup frozen peas, thawed
- 1 cup grape tomatoes, halved
- 1 cup sliced almonds, toasted

1. In a small bowl, whisk the first seven ingredients. Gradually whisk in grapeseed oil until blended.
2. In a large bowl, combine lettuces, red pepper, celery, cucumber, peas and tomatoes. Just before serving, pour dressing over salad and toss to coat. Sprinkle with almonds.
NOTE *To toast nuts, bake in a shallow pan in a 350° oven for 5-10 minutes or cook in a skillet over low heat until lightly browned, stirring occasionally.*

GERMAN APPLES

In culinary school, I had to make a salad with Granny Smith apples. I remembered my mother's German potato salad and swapped out the potatoes.

—SHARYN HILL LAS CRUCES, NM

PREP: 10 MIN. • **COOK:** 25 MIN.
MAKES: 6 SERVINGS

- 6 bacon strips, cut crosswise into ½-inch slices
- ½ cup chopped onion
- 2 tablespoons all-purpose flour
- 1 teaspoon salt
- ½ teaspoon pepper
- 1 cup water
- ½ cup cider vinegar
- ¼ cup sugar
- 5½ cups Granny Smith apples (about 4 large), cut into ½-inch slices

1. In a large skillet, cook the bacon over medium heat until crisp; drain on paper towels. Discard all but 2 tablespoons drippings. Add the onion; cook until tender, 2-3 minutes. Stir in flour, salt and pepper until blended. Add water and vinegar; cook and stir until slightly thickened, about 1 minute. Stir in sugar until dissolved.
2. Return bacon to pan; gently add apple slices. Cook, stirring constantly, until the apples are wilted and slightly caramelized, 10-12 minutes. Remove from heat; serve warm.

TEST KITCHEN TIP
Wondering how long you've got after opening a package of bacon? You can safely store it in the refrigerator for up to one week—beyond that and you should freeze it for up to one month.

GREEN BEAN-CHERRY TOMATO SALAD

My grandma made a cold green bean salad with potatoes for every family barbecue. Now I bring my own version of the recipe to parties. With the added fun of cherry tomatoes, the classic favorite is even better.

—ANGELA LEMOINE HOWELL, NJ

PREP: 25 MIN. • **COOK:** 10 MIN.
MAKES: 12 SERVINGS

- 1½ pounds fresh green beans, trimmed
- 1 pint cherry tomatoes, halved
- 1 small red onion, halved and thinly sliced
- 3 tablespoons red wine vinegar
- 1½ teaspoons sugar
- ¾ teaspoon dried oregano
- ¾ teaspoon salt
- ¼ teaspoon garlic powder
- ¼ teaspoon pepper
- ¼ cup olive oil

1. In a 6-qt. stockpot, bring 6 cups water to a boil. Add beans in batches; cook, uncovered, 2-3 minutes or just until crisp-tender. Remove the beans and immediately drop into ice water. Drain and pat dry.
2. Transfer beans to a large bowl. Add tomatoes and onion; toss to combine. In a small bowl, whisk vinegar, sugar, oregano, salt, garlic powder and pepper. Gradually whisk in oil until blended. Pour over bean mixture; toss to coat.

GREEN BEAN-CHERRY TOMATO SALAD

VIBRANT BLACK-EYED PEA SALAD

VIBRANT BLACK-EYED PEA SALAD

This black-eyed pea salad reminds me of a Southern cooking class my husband and I took while visiting Savannah, Georgia.

—**DANIELLE ULAM** HOOKSTOWN, PA

PREP: 25 MIN. + CHILLING
MAKES: 10 SERVINGS

- 2 cans (15½ ounces each) black-eyed peas, rinsed and drained
- 2 cups grape tomatoes, halved
- 1 each small green, yellow and red peppers, finely chopped
- 1 small red onion, chopped
- 1 celery rib, chopped
- 2 tablespoons minced fresh basil

DRESSING

- ¼ cup red wine vinegar or balsamic vinegar
- 1 tablespoon stone-ground mustard
- 1 teaspoon minced fresh oregano or ¼ teaspoon dried oregano
- ¾ teaspoon salt
- ½ teaspoon freshly ground pepper
- ¼ cup olive oil

1. In a large bowl, combine peas, tomatoes, peppers, onion, celery and basil.

2. For the dressing, in a small bowl, whisk vinegar, mustard, oregano, salt and pepper. Gradually whisk in oil until blended. Drizzle over the salad; toss to coat. Refrigerate, covered, at least 3 hours before serving.

RAVISHING RADISH SALAD

Showcase radishes in all their glory with a fresh, crunchy salad. Herbs and fennel take it up another notch.

—**MAGGIE RUDDY** ALTOONA, IA

PREP: 30 MIN. + CHILLING
MAKES: 6 SERVINGS

- 24 radishes, quartered
- 1 teaspoon salt
- 1 teaspoon pepper
- 6 green onions, chopped
- ½ cup thinly sliced fennel bulb
- 6 fresh basil leaves, thinly sliced
- ¼ cup snipped fresh dill
- ¼ cup olive oil
- 2 tablespoons champagne vinegar
- 2 tablespoons honey
- 2 garlic cloves, minced
- ½ cup chopped walnuts, toasted

1. Place the radishes in a large bowl. Sprinkle with salt and pepper; toss to coat. Add the onions, fennel, basil and dill. In a small bowl, whisk oil, vinegar, honey and garlic. Pour over salad and toss to coat.

2. Cover and refrigerate salad for at least 1 hour. Sprinkle with walnuts just before serving.

COMPANY GREEN SALAD

I partially assemble this salad in advance and take the remaining ingredients (candied nuts, seeds, rice noodles and dressing) to mix in at the potluck. It comes together perfectly every time!

—**JOAN HALLFORD** NORTH RICHLAND HILLS, TX

START TO FINISH: 25 MIN.
MAKES: 12 SERVINGS

- 2 teaspoons butter
- ¾ cup sliced almonds
- 1 tablespoon sugar

DRESSING
- ¼ cup canola oil
- 3 tablespoons rice vinegar
- 2 tablespoons brown sugar

SALAD
- 8 cups torn leaf lettuce
- 1 medium sweet red pepper, chopped
- 1 medium sweet yellow pepper, chopped
- 2 green onions, chopped
- 1 can (3 ounces) crispy rice noodles
- ⅓ cup sunflower kernels

1. In a small heavy skillet, melt butter. Add almonds and cook over medium heat until toasted, about 4 minutes. Sprinkle with sugar. Cook and stir for 2-3 minutes or until sugar is melted. Spread on foil to cool.
2. For dressing, in a small bowl, whisk the oil, vinegar and brown sugar. Chill until serving.
3. For salad, in a large bowl, combine the lettuce, peppers and green onions. Add dressing; toss to coat. Sprinkle with rice noodles, sunflower kernels and almonds. Serve immediately.

GOES GREAT WITH
Since this salad feeds a crowd, serve it with a super casserole, such as Chicken Cordon Bleu Bake, page 28!

FRESH SUGAR
SNAP PEA SALAD

FRESH SUGAR SNAP PEA SALAD

We found fresh sugar snap peas at the local produce market. With a quick and tasty onion dressing, they make a cheerful salad.

—**COURTNEY STULTZ** WEIR, KS

PREP: 15 MIN. + CHILLING
MAKES: 6 SERVINGS

- 2 tablespoons olive oil
- 2 tablespoons white wine vinegar
- 2 teaspoons honey
- ½ teaspoon salt
- ½ teaspoon pepper
- ¼ teaspoon dried thyme
- ½ cup chopped onion
- ½ teaspoon poppy seeds
- 1 pound fresh sugar snap peas, trimmed and halved (about 4 cups)

1. Place the first seven ingredients in a blender; cover and process until blended. Transfer to a large bowl; stir in poppy seeds.
2. Add peas to dressing and toss to coat. Refrigerate, covered, 30 minutes before serving.

TANGY POPPY SEED FRUIT SALAD

For a fruit salad that's delightful, I like to combine berries and citrus with a honey lime dressing flecked with poppy seeds.

—**CARRIE HOWELL** LEHI, UT

START TO FINISH: 20 MIN.
MAKES: 10 SERVINGS

- 1 can (20 ounces) unsweetened pineapple chunks, drained
- 1 pound fresh strawberries, quartered
- 2 cups fresh blueberries
- 2 cups fresh raspberries
- 2 medium navel oranges, peeled and sectioned
- 2 medium kiwifruit, peeled, halved and sliced

DRESSING
- 2 to 4 tablespoons honey
- ½ teaspoon grated lime peel
- 2 tablespoons lime juice
- 2 teaspoons poppy seeds

Place all fruit in a large bowl. In a small bowl, whisk the dressing ingredients. Drizzle over fruit; toss gently to combine.

BALSAMIC CUCUMBER SALAD

Serve up this fast, fresh salad at your next get-together. It makes for an easygoing side dish for kabobs, chicken or anything hot off the grill.

—BLAIR LONERGAN ROCHELLE, VA

START TO FINISH: 15 MIN.
MAKES: 6 SERVINGS

- 1 large English cucumber, halved and sliced
- 2 cups grape tomatoes, halved
- 1 medium red onion, halved and thinly sliced
- ½ cup balsamic vinaigrette
- ¾ cup crumbled reduced-fat feta cheese

In a large bowl, combine cucumber, tomatoes and onion. Add vinaigrette; toss to coat. Refrigerate, covered, until serving. Just before serving, stir in cheese. Serve with a slotted spoon.

FAST FIX▶

BLUE CHEESE APPLE SLAW

I always appreciate recipes that can be made ahead and chilled until you're ready to eat. If you want your dish to have more color, add extra carrot.

—ELIZABETH GODECKE CHICAGO, IL

START TO FINISH: 30 MIN.
MAKES: 9 SERVINGS

- ½ cup mayonnaise
- ½ cup sour cream
- ¼ cup cider vinegar
- 2 tablespoons lemon juice
- 1 tablespoon stone-ground mustard
- 2 teaspoons sugar
- ½ teaspoon salt
- ½ teaspoon pepper
- 1 medium head cabbage, shredded
- 1 medium tart apple, shredded
- 1 medium carrot, shredded
- ½ cup crumbled blue cheese

1. In a small bowl, whisk the first eight ingredients.
2. In a large bowl, combine the cabbage, apple, carrot and cheese. Pour dressing over salad; toss to coat. Cover and refrigerate until serving.

BALSAMIC CUCUMBER SALAD
Blair Lonergan
Rochelle, VA

SPINACH SALAD WITH POPPY SEED DRESSING
Nikki Barton
Providence, UT

RIBBON SALAD WITH ORANGE VINAIGRETTE

Zucchini, cucumbers and carrots are peeled into ribbons in a citrusy salad. We like to serve it on special occasions.
—NANCY HEISHMAN LAS VEGAS, NV

START TO FINISH: 30 MIN.
MAKES: 8 SERVINGS

- 1 medium zucchini
- 1 medium cucumber
- 1 medium carrot
- 3 medium oranges
- 3 cups fresh baby spinach
- 4 green onions, finely chopped
- ½ cup chopped walnuts
- ½ teaspoon salt
- ½ teaspoon pepper
- ½ cup golden raisins, optional

VINAIGRETTE
- ¼ cup olive oil
- 4 teaspoons white wine vinegar
- 1 tablespoon finely chopped green onion
- 2 teaspoons honey
- ¼ teaspoon salt
- ¼ teaspoon pepper

1. Using a vegetable peeler, shave zucchini, cucumber and carrot lengthwise into very thin strips.
2. Finely grate enough peel from oranges to measure 2 tablespoons. Cut one orange crosswise in half; squeeze juice from orange to measure ½ cup. Reserve peel and juice for vinaigrette. Cut a thin slice from the top and bottom of remaining oranges; stand oranges upright on a cutting board. With a knife, cut off peel and outer membrane from orange. Cut along the membrane of each segment to remove fruit.
3. In a large bowl, combine spinach, orange sections, green onions, walnuts, salt, pepper and, if desired, raisins. Add vegetable ribbons; gently toss to combine. In a small bowl, combine vinaigrette ingredients. Add reserved orange peel and juice; whisk until blended. Drizzle half of the vinaigrette over salad; toss to coat. Serve with remaining vinaigrette.

SPINACH SALAD WITH POPPY SEED DRESSING

I love to bring this salad to parties or wow guests at our home. It's been a family favorite for a while. The easy homemade dressing is the best part.
—NIKKI BARTON PROVIDENCE, UT

START TO FINISH: 25 MIN.
MAKES: 6 SERVINGS (1 CUP DRESSING)

- 4 cups fresh baby spinach
- 4 cups torn iceberg lettuce
- 1½ cups sliced fresh mushrooms
- ½ pound bacon strips, cooked and crumbled

DRESSING
- ¼ cup red wine vinegar
- ¼ cup chopped red onion
- 3 tablespoons sugar
- ¾ teaspoon salt
- ¼ teaspoon ground mustard
- ½ cup canola oil
- 1½ teaspoons poppy seeds

1. In a large bowl, combine spinach, lettuce, mushrooms and bacon. Place the vinegar, onion, sugar, salt and mustard in blender. While processing, gradually add oil in a steady stream. Transfer to a bowl; stir in poppy seeds.
2. Divide salad among six plates; drizzle with dressing.

RIBBON SALAD WITH ORANGE VINAIGRETTE

BEET SALAD WITH LEMON DRESSING

I was looking for a recipe for pickled beets and saw one that used lemon instead of vinegar. I immediately thought of making a tabbouleh-inspired salad with beets instead of tomatoes.

—ANN SHEEHY LAWRENCE, MA

PREP: 10 MIN. • **BAKE:** 1¼ HOURS
MAKES: 6 SERVINGS

- 3 medium fresh beets (about 1 pound)
- 1 cup finely chopped English cucumber
- 6 green onions, thinly sliced
- ½ cup shredded carrot
- ½ cup chopped sweet yellow or red pepper
- ¼ cup finely chopped red onion
- ¼ cup finely chopped radish
- ¾ cup minced fresh parsley

DRESSING

- 3 tablespoons olive oil
- 2 teaspoons grated lemon peel
- 3 tablespoons lemon juice
- 1 garlic clove, minced
- ¼ teaspoon salt
- ¼ teaspoon pepper

Preheat oven to 400°. Scrub beets and trim tops. Wrap beets in foil; place on a baking sheet. Bake until tender, 1¼-1½ hours. Cool slightly. Peel beets and cut into cubes.

1. Place the remaining vegetables and the parsley in a large bowl. Whisk together dressing ingredients; toss with the cucumber mixture. Gently stir in beets.

GOES **GREAT** WITH

Goat cheese really complements the flavor of beets, so we suggest serving some on the side with crackers for a light, breezy meal.

ROASTED APPLE SALAD WITH SPICY MAPLE-CIDER VINAIGRETTE

ROASTED APPLE SALAD WITH SPICY MAPLE-CIDER VINAIGRETTE

We bought loads of apples and needed to use them. To help the flavors come alive, I roasted the apples and tossed them with a sweet dressing.

—JANICE ELDER CHARLOTTE, NC

PREP: 15 MIN. • **BAKE:** 20 MIN. + COOLING
MAKES: 8 SERVINGS

- 4 medium Fuji, Gala or other firm apples, quartered
- 2 tablespoons olive oil

DRESSING

- 2 tablespoons cider vinegar
- 2 tablespoons olive oil
- 1 tablespoon maple syrup
- 1 teaspoon Sriracha Asian hot chili sauce
- ½ teaspoon salt
- ¼ teaspoon pepper

SALAD

- 1 package (5 ounces) spring mix salad greens
- 4 pitted dates, quartered
- 1 log (4 ounces) fresh goat cheese, crumbled
- ½ cup chopped pecans, toasted

1. Preheat oven to 375°. Place apples in a foil-lined 15x10x1-in. baking pan; drizzle with oil and toss to coat. Roast 20-30 minutes or until tender, stirring occasionally. Cool completely.

2. In a small bowl, whisk dressing ingredients until blended. In a large bowl, combine the salad greens and dates. Drizzle the dressing over salad and toss to coat.

3. Divide the mixture among eight plates. Top with goat cheese and roasted apples; sprinkle with pecans. Serve immediately.

NOTE *To toast nuts, bake in a shallow pan in a 350° oven for 5-10 minutes or cook in a skillet over low heat until lightly browned, stirring occasionally.*

GRILLED FIRECRACKER POTATO SALAD

I can eat potato salad all the time. A little spice is nice, and cayenne and paprika bring the fireworks to this grilled salad.
—ASHLEY ARMSTRONG KINGSLAND, GA

PREP: 20 MIN. • **GRILL:** 20 MIN. + CHILLING
MAKES: 16 SERVINGS (1 CUP EACH)

- 3 pounds small red potatoes (about 30), quartered
- 2 tablespoons olive oil
- 1 teaspoon salt
- ½ teaspoon pepper

DRESSING
- 1½ cups mayonnaise
- ½ cup finely chopped onion
- ¼ cup Dijon mustard
- 2 tablespoons sweet pickle relish
- ½ teaspoon paprika
- ¼ teaspoon cayenne pepper

SALAD
- 6 hard-cooked large eggs, chopped
- 2 celery ribs, finely chopped
  Minced fresh chives, optional

1. Toss potatoes with oil, salt and pepper; place in a grill wok or basket. Grill, covered, over medium heat 20-25 minutes or until potatoes are tender, stirring occasionally. Transfer potatoes to a large bowl; cool slightly.
2. In a small bowl, mix dressing ingredients. Add dressing, eggs and celery to potatoes; toss to combine. Refrigerate, covered, 1-2 hours or until cold. If desired, sprinkle salad with chives.
NOTE *If you do not have a grill wok or basket, use a large disposable foil pan and poke holes in the bottom of the pan.*

GRILLED FIRECRACKER POTATO SALAD

SOUTHERN CORN BREAD SALAD

When it's time to feed a crowd, I make an eye-popping corn bread salad. Beautiful in a trifle bowl, it tastes like instant sunshine by the spoonful.
—DEBBIE JOHNSON CENTERTOWN, MO

PREP: 30 MIN. + CHILLING
MAKES: 16 SERVINGS (¾ CUP EACH)

- 1 package (8½ ounces) corn bread/ muffin mix
- 1 cup (8 ounces) sour cream
- 1 cup mayonnaise
- 1 envelope ranch salad dressing mix
- 3 large tomatoes, seeded and chopped
- ½ cup chopped sweet red pepper
- ½ cup chopped green pepper
- 1 cup thinly sliced green onions, divided
- 2 cans (15 ounces each) pinto beans, rinsed and drained
- 2 cups (8 ounces) shredded cheddar cheese
- 10 bacon strips, cooked and crumbled
- 3½ cups frozen corn, thawed

1. Prepare and bake corn bread mix according to package directions, using an 8-in. square baking dish. Crumble when cool.
2. Mix sour cream, mayonnaise and salad dressing mix until blended. In a separate bowl, combine tomatoes, peppers and ½ cup green onions.
3. In a 3-qt. glass bowl, layer half of each: corn bread, beans, tomato mixture, cheese, bacon, corn and dressing. Repeat layers. Top with remaining green onions. Refrigerate 3 hours.

★ ★ ★ ★ ★ **READER REVIEW**

"Great salad. I've been making this for years. Sometimes I sub chili beans for the pinto beans, and I usually eliminate the bacon to make it vegetarian."
MS11145 TASTEOFHOME.COM

HONEY-LEMON
ASPARAGUS

Side Dishes

Finding the right side to pair with a main dish (and dessert) can feel almost as lucky as discovering a pot of gold. The good news? These delicious options are ready to become your next big find!

FAST FIX

HONEY-LEMON ASPARAGUS

Everyone who tastes my glazed asparagus takes seconds, so I double the recipe. For another option, try root veggies like turnip and parsnip.
—**LORRAINE CALAND** SHUNIAH, ON

START TO FINISH: 15 MIN.
MAKES: 8 SERVINGS

- 2 **pounds fresh asparagus, trimmed**
- ¼ **cup honey**
- 2 **tablespoons butter**
- 2 **tablespoons lemon juice**
- 1 **teaspoon sea salt**
- 1 **teaspoon balsamic vinegar**
- 1 **teaspoon Worcestershire sauce**

1. In a large saucepan, bring 8 cups water to a boil. Add the asparagus in batches; cook, uncovered, 1-2 minutes or just until crisp-tender. Drain and pat dry.
2. Meanwhile, in a small saucepan, combine the remaining ingredients. Bring to a boil. Reduce the heat; simmer, uncovered, 2 minutes or until slightly thickened.
3. Transfer asparagus to a large bowl; drizzle with glaze and toss gently to coat.

GOES **GREAT** WITH

There's lots to love about asparagus! It shines as a side, it can be cooked many different ways, and it complements almost any meat main dish.

SLOW COOKER

SLOW COOKER SPINACH & RICE

I started making this in the slow cooker to save oven space during the holidays. It's so convenient, I no longer reserve it for special occasions!
—**ERICA POLLY** SUN PRAIRIE, WI

PREP: 20 MIN. • **COOK:** 3 HOURS + STANDING
MAKES: 8 SERVINGS

- 2 **tablespoons butter**
- 1 **medium onion, finely chopped**
- 2 **garlic cloves, minced**
- ¼ **teaspoon dried thyme**
- 4 **cups reduced-sodium chicken broth**
- 2 **packages (10 ounces each) frozen chopped spinach, thawed and squeezed dry**
- 1 **package (8 ounces) cream cheese, softened**
- 1 **teaspoon salt**
- 1 **teaspoon pepper**
- 2 **cups uncooked converted rice**
- 8 **ounces cheddar cheese, shredded**
- ½ **cup panko (Japanese) bread crumbs**
- ¼ **cup grated Parmesan cheese**

1. In a large saucepan, melt butter over medium heat. Add onion; cook and stir 4-6 minutes or until tender. Add garlic and thyme; cook 1 minute longer. Add broth; bring to a simmer. Remove from heat. Stir in spinach, cream cheese, salt and pepper until blended. Transfer to a 4-qt. slow cooker. Stir in rice.
2. Cook, covered, 3-4 hours or until rice is tender and liquid is absorbed, stirring halfway through cooking. Remove the insert; top with cheddar cheese. Let it stand, covered, for 20 minutes. Top with bread crumbs and Parmesan cheese.

BUTTERNUT SQUASH
& POTATO MASH

BUTTERNUT SQUASH & POTATO MASH

Some people like squash, some people like potatoes. Mash the two together, and you've got true food love! This is a smart, tricky way to get kids to eat their veggies.
—JASMINE ROSE CRYSTAL LAKE, IL

PREP: 25 MIN. • **COOK:** 20 MIN.
MAKES: 10 SERVINGS (¾ CUP EACH)

- 8 cups cubed peeled butternut squash (about 4 pounds)
- 4 cups cubed peeled potatoes (about 4 medium)
- 16 garlic cloves, peeled
- 2 tablespoons sesame seeds
- 1 teaspoon ground cumin
- 1 cup shredded Colby-Monterey Jack cheese
- 2 tablespoons butter
- 1½ teaspoons salt
- ½ teaspoon pepper

1. Place squash, potatoes and garlic in a Dutch oven; add water to cover. Bring to a boil. Reduce heat; cook, uncovered, 10-15 minutes or until tender.

2. Meanwhile, in a dry small skillet, toast sesame seeds and cumin over medium-low heat 3-4 minutes or until aromatic, stirring frequently. Remove from heat.

3. Drain squash mixture. Mash the vegetables, adding the cheese, butter, salt and pepper. Sprinkle with sesame seed mixture.

SLOW COOKER 🍲
MAPLE-WALNUT SWEET POTATOES

Sweet potatoes with dried cherries and walnuts make this side just so delectable.
—SARAH HERSE BROOKLYN, NY

PREP: 15 MIN. • **COOK:** 5 HOURS
MAKES: 12 SERVINGS (¾ CUP EACH)

- 4 pounds sweet potatoes (about 8 medium)
- ¾ cup coarsely chopped walnuts, divided
- ½ cup packed light brown sugar
- ½ cup dried cherries, coarsely chopped
- ½ cup maple syrup
- ¼ cup apple cider or juice
- ¼ teaspoon salt

1. Peel and cut the sweet potatoes lengthwise in half; cut crosswise into ½-in. slices. Place them in a 5-qt. slow cooker. Add ½ cup walnuts, brown sugar, cherries, syrup, cider and salt; toss to combine.

2. Cook, covered, on low 5-6 hours or until potatoes are tender. Sprinkle with remaining walnuts.

GOES GREAT WITH
You'll want to balance out this sweet side with something more savory, like Almond Turkey Casserole on page 30.

SLOW COOKER
ORANGE SPICE CARROTS

In order to get my son to eat his veggies, I mix and match flavors and spices. My slow cooker carrots with orange and cinnamon have him hooked.

—**CHRISTINA ADDISON** BLANCHESTER, OH

PREP: 10 MIN. • **COOK:** 4 HOURS
MAKES: 6 SERVINGS

- 2 pounds medium carrots or baby carrots, cut into 1-inch pieces
- ½ cup packed brown sugar
- ½ cup orange juice
- 2 tablespoons butter
- ¾ teaspoon ground cinnamon
- ½ teaspoon salt
- ¼ teaspoon ground nutmeg
- 4 teaspoons cornstarch
- ¼ cup cold water

1. In a 3-qt. slow cooker, combine the first seven ingredients. Cook, covered, on low 4-5 hours or until the carrots are tender.

2. In a small bowl, mix cornstarch and water until smooth; gradually stir into carrot mixture until sauce is thickened.

SLOW COOKER
GARLIC GREEN BEANS WITH GORGONZOLA

I updated this green bean holiday side dish by adding a touch of white wine, fresh thyme and green onions. It's delicious and simple to make, and my family loves it!

—**NANCY HEISHMAN** LAS VEGAS, NV

PREP: 20 MIN. • **COOK:** 3 HOURS
MAKES: 10 SERVINGS

- 2 pounds fresh green beans, trimmed and halved
- 1 can (8 ounces) sliced water chestnuts, drained
- 4 green onions, chopped
- 5 bacon strips, cooked and crumbled, divided
- ⅓ cup white wine or chicken broth
- 2 tablespoons minced fresh thyme or 2 teaspoons dried thyme
- 4 garlic cloves, minced
- 1½ teaspoons seasoned salt
- 1 cup (8 ounces) sour cream
- ¾ cup crumbled Gorgonzola cheese

1. Place green beans, water chestnuts, green onions and ¼ cup cooked bacon in a 4-qt. slow cooker. In a small bowl, mix wine, thyme, garlic and seasoned salt; pour over top. Cook, covered, on low 3-4 hours or until green beans are crisp-tender. Drain liquid from beans.

2. Just before serving, stir in the sour cream; sprinkle with cheese and the remaining bacon.

⑤ INGREDIENTS FAST FIX
BALSAMIC ZUCCHINI SAUTE

This fast veggie dish is flavorful and only uses a few ingredients, making it easy to whip up while your entree is cooking.

—**ELIZABETH BRAMKAMP** GIG HARBOR, WA

START TO FINISH: 20 MIN
MAKES: 4 SERVINGS

- 1 tablespoon olive oil
- 3 medium zucchini, cut into thin slices
- ½ cup chopped sweet onion
- ½ teaspoon salt
- ½ teaspoon dried rosemary, crushed
- ¼ teaspoon pepper
- 2 tablespoons balsamic vinegar
- ⅓ cup crumbled feta cheese

In a large skillet, heat the oil over medium-high heat; saute zucchini and onion until crisp-tender, 6-8 minutes. Stir in the seasonings. Add the vinegar; cook and stir 2 minutes. Top with cheese.

✳

TEST KITCHEN TIP
Want to store your sweet onions for longer-term use? Freeze 'em! Chop the onions and place them on a 15x10x1-inch pan, then put the pan in the freezer. Once the chopped onions are frozen, transfer them to freezer bags or into containers. You can store sweet onions this way for up to one year!

ORANGE SPICE CARROTS

MOM'S APPLE CORN BREAD STUFFING

My speedy recipe is end-all be-all stuffing in our family. We never have leftovers.

—MARIE FORTE RARITAN, NJ

PREP: 15 MIN. • **BAKE:** 35 MIN.
MAKES: 16 SERVINGS

- 6 large Granny Smith apples, peeled and chopped
- 1 package (14 ounces) crushed corn bread stuffing
- ½ cup butter, melted
- 1 can (14½ ounces) chicken broth

1. Preheat oven to 350°. Combine apples, stuffing and melted butter. Add broth; mix well.
2. Transfer to a greased 13x9-in. baking dish. Bake until golden brown, 35-40 minutes.

OVEN-DRIED TOMATOES

I had 100 tomato varieties to work with from our greenhouse, so I started oven-drying them with much success.

—SUE GRONHOLZ BEAVER DAM, WI

PREP: 15 MIN. • **BAKE:** 5 HOURS
MAKES: 4 SERVINGS

- 8 plum tomatoes
  Ice water
- ¼ cup olive oil
- ¼ cup minced fresh basil
- 4 garlic cloves, minced
- ½ teaspoon salt
- ¼ teaspoon pepper

1. Preheat the oven to 250°. Fill a large saucepan two-thirds with water; bring to a boil. Cut a shallow "X" on the bottom of each tomato. Place the tomatoes, a few at a time, in boiling water just until the skin at the "X" begins to loosen, about 30 seconds. Remove and immediately drop into ice water. Pull off and discard skins.
2. Cut tomatoes in half lengthwise. Combine all ingredients; toss to coat. Transfer tomatoes, cut side up, to a greased 15x10x1-in. baking pan. Roast until tomatoes are soft and slightly shriveled, about 5 hours. Cool it completely; refrigerate.

RED CABBAGE WITH BACON

RED CABBAGE WITH BACON

If you have braised, marinated or served red cabbage raw, try it steamed, then toss with bacon and a tangy sauce. We serve this with pork or chicken.

—SHERRI MELOTIK OAK CREEK, WI

START TO FINISH: 25 MIN.
MAKES: 6 SERVINGS

- 1 medium head red cabbage (about 2 pounds), shredded
- 8 bacon strips, chopped
- 1 small onion, quartered and thinly sliced
- 2 tablespoons all-purpose flour
- ¼ cup packed brown sugar
- ½ cup water
- ¼ cup cider vinegar
- 1 teaspoon salt
- ⅛ teaspoon pepper

1. In a large saucepan, place steamer basket over 1 in. of water. Place the cabbage in basket. Bring water to a boil. Reduce the heat to maintain a simmer; steam, covered, 6-8 minutes or just until tender.
2. Meanwhile, in a large skillet, cook the bacon over medium heat until crisp, stirring occasionally. Remove it with a slotted spoon; drain on paper towels. Then discard the drippings, reserving 2 tablespoons in pan.
3. Add onion to the drippings; cook and stir over medium-high heat, about 4-6 minutes or until tender. Stir in the flour and brown sugar until blended. Gradually stir in water and vinegar. Bring to a boil, stirring constantly; cook and stir 1-2 minutes or until thickened. Stir in cabbage, bacon, salt and pepper.

SLOW COOKER

SIMPLE VEGETARIAN SLOW-COOKED BEANS

When I'm faced with a hungry family to feed, these tasty beans with spinach, tomatoes and carrots are a go-to dish.

—**JENNIFER REID** FARMINGTON, ME

PREP: 15 MIN. • **COOK:** 4 HOURS
MAKES: 8 SERVINGS

- 4 **cans (15½ ounces each) great northern beans, rinsed and drained**
- 4 **medium carrots, finely chopped (about 2 cups)**
- 1 **cup vegetable stock**
- 6 **garlic cloves, minced**
- 2 **teaspoons ground cumin**
- ¾ **teaspoon salt**
- ⅛ **teaspoon chili powder**
- 4 **cups fresh baby spinach, coarsely chopped**
- 1 **cup oil-packed sun-dried tomatoes, patted dry and chopped**
- ⅓ **cup minced fresh cilantro**
- ⅓ **cup minced fresh parsley**

In a 3-qt. slow cooker, combine the first seven ingredients. Cook, covered, on low 4-5 hours or until carrots are tender, adding spinach and tomatoes during the last 10 minutes of cooking. Stir in cilantro and parsley.

★ ★ ★ ★ ★ **READER REVIEW**

"I didn't have 4 cans of beans for this recipe, so I made my own using 1 pound of cooked beans. I added the listed veggies and seasonings, but increased the vegetables by adding 1 medium onion, 1 cup bell (tri-color) pepper, 2 ribs celery, 1 jalapeno, and 1 small zucchini."

ANNRMS TASTEOFHOME.COM

SIMPLE VEGETARIAN SLOW-COOKED BEANS

SUMMER ORZO

I'm always looking for fun ways to use the fresh veggies that come in my Community Supported Agriculture box, and this salad is one of my favorite creations. I like to improvise with whatever I have on hand, so feel free to do the same here!

—**SHAYNA MARMAR** PHILADELPHIA, PA

PREP: 30 MIN. + CHILLING
MAKES: 16 SERVINGS (¾ CUP EACH)

- 1   **package (16 ounces) orzo pasta**
- ¼   **cup water**
- 1½ **cups fresh or frozen corn**
- 24 **cherry tomatoes, halved**
- 2   **cups crumbled feta cheese**
- 1   **medium cucumber, seeded and chopped**
- 1   **small red onion, finely chopped**
- ¼   **cup minced fresh mint**
- 2   **tablespoons capers, drained and chopped, optional**
- ½   **cup olive oil**
- ¼   **cup lemon juice**
- 1   **tablespoon grated lemon peel**
- 1½ **teaspoons salt**
- 1   **teaspoon pepper**
- 1   **cup sliced almonds, toasted**

1. Cook orzo according to package directions for al dente. Drain orzo; rinse with cold water and drain well. Transfer to a large bowl.
2. In a large nonstick skillet, heat water over medium heat. Add corn; cook and stir 3-4 minutes or until crisp-tender. Add to the orzo; stir in the tomatoes, feta cheese, cucumber, onion, mint and, if desired, the capers. In a small bowl, whisk the oil, lemon juice, lemon peel, salt and pepper until blended. Pour over orzo mixture; toss to coat. Refrigerate 30 minutes.
3. Just before serving, stir in almonds.

TEST KITCHEN TIP
Why go to the trouble of toasting nuts for a recipe? There are two good reasons: flavor and appearance. Toasting nuts intensifies the flavor while also giving them a prettier appearance, which can be especially desirable when they are topping dishes.

ROASTED TATER ROUNDS WITH GREEN ONIONS & TARRAGON

ROASTED TATER ROUNDS WITH GREEN ONIONS & TARRAGON

I am crazy for potatoes, especially when they're roasted and toasted. Toss them with fresh herbs and green onions for a bold finish.

—**ALLY PHILLIPS** MURRELLS INLET, SC

PREP: 25 MIN. • **BROIL:** 10 MIN.
MAKES: 8 SERVINGS

- 4 **pounds potatoes (about 8 medium), sliced ¼ inch thick**
    Cooking spray
- 2 **teaspoons sea salt**
- 1 **teaspoon coarsely ground pepper**
- 6 **green onions, thinly sliced (about ¾ cup)**
- 3 **tablespoons minced fresh parsley**
- 2 **tablespoons minced fresh tarragon**
    Olive oil, optional

1. Preheat the broiler. Place potatoes in a large microwave-safe bowl; spritz with cooking spray and toss them to coat. Microwave, covered, on high 10-12 minutes or until almost tender, stirring halfway through cooking.
2. Spread the potatoes into greased 15x10x1-in. baking pans. Spritz with additional cooking spray; sprinkle with salt and pepper.
3. Broil 4-6 in. from heat for 10-12 minutes or until they are golden brown, stirring halfway through cooking. In a small bowl, mix green onions, parsley and tarragon. Sprinkle over potatoes; toss to coat. If desired, drizzle with olive oil.

SCALLOPED POTATOES WITH MUSHROOMS

Potatoes and mushrooms create a one-dish option I absolutely love. Give it a try and you'll see what I mean!
—COURTNEY STULTZ WEIR, KS

PREP: 40 MIN. • **BAKE:** 15 MIN. + STANDING
MAKES: 8 SERVINGS

- 2 pounds potatoes (about 4 medium), peeled and sliced
- 1 tablespoon butter
- ½ pound sliced fresh mushrooms
- 1 small onion, chopped
- 1 garlic clove, minced
- ¼ cup all-purpose flour
- 1 cup chicken broth
- 1 teaspoon salt
- ½ teaspoon dried oregano
- ½ teaspoon pepper
- 1 cup (8 ounces) sour cream
- 1 cup coarsely chopped fresh spinach
- 2 cups shredded Swiss cheese

1. Preheat the oven to 375°. Place the potatoes in a large saucepan; add the water to cover. Bring to a boil. Reduce heat; cook, uncovered, 8-12 minutes or until tender. Drain.
2. Meanwhile, in another saucepan, heat butter over medium-high heat. Add mushrooms and onion; cook and stir 6-8 minutes or until tender. Stir in garlic; cook 1 minute longer.
3. In a small bowl, whisk flour, broth and seasonings until smooth; stir into the mushroom mixture. Bring it to a boil, stirring constantly; cook and stir for 1-2 minutes or until the sauce is thickened. Remove from heat; stir in sour cream.
4. Arrange half of the potatoes in a greased 1½-qt. or 8-in. square baking dish; top with spinach. Spread half of the hot mushroom sauce over the top; sprinkle with 1 cup cheese. Layer with remaining potatoes, sauce and cheese.
5. Bake, uncovered, 12-15 minutes or until heated through and cheese is melted. Let stand for 10 minutes before serving.

FAST FIX
ROASTED GREEN BEANS WITH LEMON & WALNUTS

I first tasted roasted green beans at a restaurant and fell in love with the texture and flavor. This is my personal take and it's always a big hit at our family table.
—LILY JULOW LAWRENCEVILLE, GA

START TO FINISH: 25 MIN.
MAKES: 8 SERVINGS

- 2 pounds fresh green beans, trimmed
- 2 shallots, thinly sliced
- 6 garlic cloves, crushed
- 2 tablespoons olive oil
- ¾ teaspoon salt
- ¼ teaspoon pepper
- 2 teaspoons grated lemon peel
- ½ cup chopped walnuts, toasted

1. Preheat oven to 425°. In a large bowl, combine green beans, shallots and garlic; drizzle the mix with olive oil and sprinkle with salt and pepper. Transfer to two 15x10x1-in. baking pans coated with cooking spray.
2. Roast 15-20 minutes or until the beans are tender and lightly browned, stirring occasionally. Remove from oven; stir in 1 teaspoon lemon peel. Sprinkle with walnuts and remaining lemon peel.
NOTE *To toast nuts, bake in a shallow pan in a 350° oven for 5-10 minutes or cook in a skillet over low heat until lightly browned, stirring occasionally.*

ROASTED GREEN BEANS WITH LEMON & WALNUTS

JEN'S BAKED BEANS
Jennifer Heasley
York, PA

JEN'S BAKED BEANS

My daughters wanted baked beans, so I gave homemade ones a shot. With mustard, molasses and a dash of heat, I made these beans absolutely irresistible.
—**JENNIFER HEASLEY** YORK, PA

PREP: 20 MIN. • **BAKE:** 50 MIN.
MAKES: 8 SERVINGS

- **6 bacon strips, chopped**
- **4 cans (15½ ounces each) great northern beans, rinsed and drained**
- **1⅓ cups ketchup**
- **⅔ cup packed brown sugar**
- **⅓ cup molasses**
- **3 tablespoons yellow mustard**
- **2½ teaspoons garlic powder**
- **1½ teaspoons hot pepper sauce**
- **¼ teaspoon crushed red pepper flakes**

1. Preheat the oven to 325°. In an ovenproof Dutch oven, cook bacon over medium heat until it is crisp, stirring occasionally. Remove with a slotted spoon; drain on paper towels. Discard drippings.

2. Return the bacon to the pan. Stir in remaining ingredients; bring to a boil. Place in oven; bake, covered, for 50-60 minutes to allow flavors to blend.

FREEZE OPTION *Freeze cooled baked beans in freezer containers. To use the beans, partially thaw in the refrigerator overnight. Heat through in a saucepan, stirring occasionally and adding a little broth or water if necessary.*

CREAM CHEESE MASHED POTATOES

1 package (16 ounces) small pasta shells
1 cup shredded provolone cheese
1 cup shredded manchego or Monterey Jack cheese
1 cup shredded white cheddar cheese
8 bacon strips, cooked and crumbled

1. In a large bowl, whisk the first six ingredients until blended. Stir in pasta and cheeses; transfer to a 4- or 5-qt. slow cooker.
2. Cook, covered, on low 3-3½ hours or until pasta is tender. Turn off slow cooker; remove the insert. Let stand, uncovered, 15 minutes before serving. Top with bacon.

ROASTED CARROTS & FENNEL

This colorful combo is a fresh take on one of my mother's standard wintertime dishes. I usually add more carrots—as many as the pans will hold.
—LILY JULOW LAWRENCEVILLE, GA

PREP: 15 MIN. • **BAKE:** 40 MIN.
MAKES: 8 SERVINGS

2½ pounds medium carrots, peeled and cut in half lengthwise
1 large fennel bulb, cut into ½-inch wedges
1 large red onion, cut into ½-inch wedges
1 medium lemon, thinly sliced
¼ cup olive oil
2 teaspoons ground coriander
1 teaspoon ground cumin
½ teaspoon salt
¼ teaspoon pepper
   Thinly sliced fresh basil leaves

1. Preheat oven to 375°. In a large bowl, combine carrots, fennel, onion and lemon. Mix oil, coriander, cumin, salt and pepper; drizzle over carrot mixture and toss to coat. Transfer to two foil-lined 15x10x1-in. baking pans.
2. Roast 40-50 minutes or until vegetables are tender, stirring occasionally. Sprinkle with basil.

---

⑤ INGREDIENTS

CREAM CHEESE MASHED POTATOES

When I serve this mash, the bowl is always scraped clean. Before a big feast, I make it early and keep it warm in a slow cooker so I can focus on last-minute details.
—JILL THOMAS WASHINGTON, IN

PREP: 20 MIN. • **COOK:** 15 MIN.
MAKES: 20 SERVINGS

8 pounds russet potatoes
1 package (8 ounces) cream cheese, softened
½ cup butter, melted
2 teaspoons salt
¾ teaspoon pepper
   Additional melted butter, optional
¼ cup finely chopped green onions

1. Peel and cube the potatoes. Place in a large stockpot; add water to cover. Bring to a boil. Reduce the heat; cook, uncovered, until tender, about 12-15 minutes. Drain.

2. With a mixer, beat cream cheese, ½ cup melted butter, salt and pepper until smooth. Add potatoes; beat until light and fluffy. If desired, top with additional melted butter. Sprinkle with green onions.

SLOW COOKER 🍲

SLOW COOKER BACON MAC & CHEESE

I'm all about easy slow cooker meals. Using more cheese than ever, I've developed an addictive spin on this casserole favorite.
—KRISTEN HEIGL STATEN ISLAND, NY

PREP: 20 MIN.
COOK: 3 HOURS + STANDING
MAKES: 18 SERVINGS (½ CUP EACH)

2 large eggs, lightly beaten
4 cups whole milk
1 can (12 ounces) evaporated milk
¼ cup butter, melted
1 tablespoon all-purpose flour
1 teaspoon salt

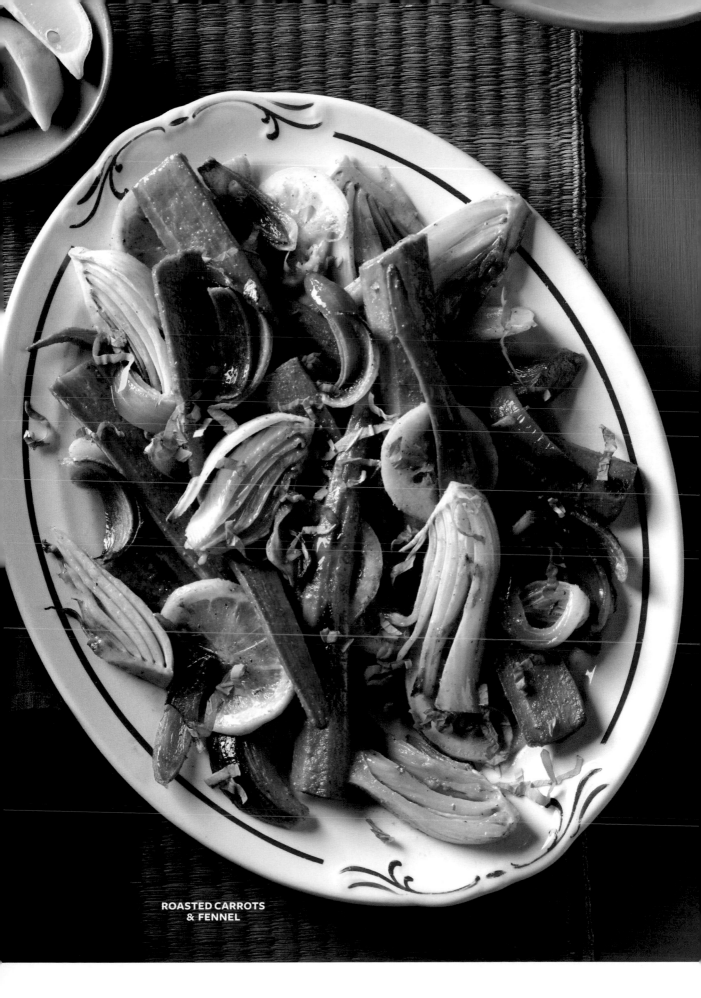

ROASTED CARROTS
& FENNEL

ORANGE-GLAZED CARROTS, ONIONS & RADISHES

Carrots and radishes give color and crunch to this sweet, spicy side. If you make it ahead, reheat and add walnuts just before serving.
—THOMAS FAGLON SOMERSET, NJ

PREP: 15 MIN. • **COOK:** 20 MIN.
MAKES: 8 SERVINGS

- 1 pound fresh pearl onions
- ¼ cup butter, cubed
- 2 pounds medium carrots, thinly sliced
- 12 radishes, thinly sliced
- ½ cup dark brown sugar
- 4 teaspoons grated orange peel
- ½ cup orange juice
- 1 cup chopped walnuts, toasted

1. In a large saucepan, bring 4 cups water to a boil. Add pearl onions; boil 3 minutes. Drain and rinse with cold water. Peel.

2. In a large skillet, heat butter over medium heat. Add the carrots, pearl onions, radishes, brown sugar, orange peel and juice; cook, covered, 10-15 minutes or until the vegetables are tender, stirring occasionally. Cook, uncovered, 5-7 minutes longer or until slightly thickened. Sprinkle with walnuts.

NOTE *To toast nuts, bake in a shallow pan in a 350° oven for 5-10 minutes or cook in a skillet over low heat until lightly browned, stirring occasionally.*

TEST KITCHEN TIP
Dark brown sugar has a more intense molasses flavor, giving this veggie-filled side a nice boost of sweetness. If you'd prefer to scale back the sweet a bit, you can use light brown sugar instead.

ROASTED BALSAMIC BRUSSELS SPROUTS WITH PANCETTA

I always loved Brussels sprouts when I was growing up, so I decided as an adult to bring them home to our family table. I've been making them ever since.
—BRENDA WASHNOCK NEGAUNEE, MI

PREP: 15 MIN. • **BAKE:** 30 MIN.
MAKES: 6 SERVINGS

- 2 pounds fresh Brussels sprouts, trimmed and halved
- 3 tablespoons olive oil, divided
- ½ teaspoon salt
- ¼ teaspoon pepper
- 2 ounces sliced pancetta or bacon strips, chopped
- 2 garlic cloves, minced
- 1 tablespoon balsamic vinegar
- ⅓ cup dried cranberries
- ½ cup pine nuts, toasted

1. Preheat the oven to 400°. Place the Brussels sprouts in a 15x10x1-in. baking pan; toss with 2 tablespoons oil, salt and pepper. Roast for 30-35 minutes or until lightly charred and tender, stirring halfway.

2. Meanwhile, in a large skillet, heat the remaining oil over medium-high heat. Add the pancetta; cook and stir 4-6 minutes or until crisp. Add garlic; cook 1 minute longer. Remove from heat; stir in vinegar.

3. In a large bowl, combine Brussels sprouts, cranberries and pancetta mixture; toss to combine. Sprinkle with pine nuts.

NOTE *To toast nuts, bake in a shallow pan in a 350° oven for 5-10 minutes or cook in a skillet over low heat until lightly browned, stirring occasionally.*

ROASTED BALSAMIC BRUSSELS SPROUTS WITH PANCETTA

SMOKY WHITE BEANS & HAM

SMOKY WHITE BEANS & HAM

I had never made or eaten this dish before meeting my husband here in Kentucky. Now I make it at least once a week. I serve it alongside some homemade sweet corn bread. Delicious!

—**CHRISTINE DUFFY** STURGIS, KY

PREP: 15 MIN. + SOAKING • **COOK:** 6 HOURS
MAKES: 10 SERVINGS

- 1 **pound dried great northern beans**
- 3 **smoked ham hocks**
- 1 **large onion, chopped**
- 3 **cans (14½ ounces each) reduced-sodium chicken or beef broth**
- 2 **cups water**
- 1 **tablespoon onion powder**
- 1 **tablespoon garlic powder**
- 2 **teaspoons pepper**
  Thinly sliced green onions, optional

1. Rinse and sort beans; soak according to package directions.

2. Drain and rinse beans, discarding liquid. Transfer beans to a 6-qt. slow cooker. Add ham hocks. Stir in onion, broth, water and seasonings. Cook, covered, on low 6-8 hours or until beans are tender.

3. Remove meat from bones when cool enough to handle; cut the ham into small pieces and return to slow cooker. Serve with a slotted spoon. Sprinkle with onions if desired.

ZUCCHINI ONION PIE

We have a lot of zucchini on hand when it's in season. This is a great and different way to use the large amounts.

—**LUCIA JOHNSON** MASSENA, NY

START TO FINISH: 30 MIN.
MAKES: 6 SERVINGS

- 3 **large eggs**
- 1 **cup grated Parmesan cheese**
- ½ **cup canola oil**
- 1 **tablespoon minced fresh parsley**
- 1 **garlic clove, minced**
- ¼ **teaspoon salt**
- ⅛ **teaspoon pepper**
- 3 **cups sliced zucchini**
- 1 **cup biscuit/baking mix**
- 1 **small onion, chopped**

In a large bowl, whisk the first seven ingredients. Stir in the zucchini, baking mix and onion. Pour into a greased 9-in. deep-dish pie plate. Bake at 350° for 25-35 minutes or until lightly browned.

SLOW COOKER CREAMED CORN WITH BACON

Every time we take this super rich corn to a potluck or work party, we leave with an empty slow cooker. It's decadent, homey and so worth the splurge.

—**MELISSA PELKEY HASS** WALESKA, GA

PREP: 10 MIN. • **COOK:** 4 HOURS
MAKES: 20 SERVINGS (½ CUP EACH)

- 10 **cups frozen corn (about 50 ounces), thawed**
- 3 **packages (8 ounces each) cream cheese, cubed**
- ½ **cup 2% milk**
- ½ **cup heavy whipping cream**
- ½ **cup butter, melted**
- ¼ **cup sugar**
- 2 **teaspoons salt**
- ¼ **teaspoon pepper**
- 4 **bacon strips, cooked and crumbled**
  Chopped green onions

In a 5-qt. slow cooker, combine the first eight ingredients. Cook, covered, on low for 4-5 hours or until heated through. Stir it just before serving. Sprinkle with bacon and green onions.

GOES GREAT WITH

Keep the bacon theme going when you bring out Bacon Chocolate Chip Cheesecake Blondies, page 95.

Soups & Breads

Few things go better together than a slice of warm homemade bread and a bowl of piping hot soup. Bring that bistro feel into your own kitchen when you prepare any of these options.

CRUSTY HOMEMADE BREAD

(5)INGREDIENTS
CRUSTY HOMEMADE BREAD

Crackling homemade bread makes an average day extraordinary. Enjoy this beautiful loaf as is, or stir in a few favorites like cheese, garlic, herbs and dried fruits.
—**MEGUMI GARCIA** MILWAUKEE, WI

PREP: 20 MIN. + RISING
BAKE: 50 MIN. + COOLING
MAKES: 1 LOAF (16 SLICES)

- 1½ **teaspoons active dry yeast**
- 1¾ **cups water (70° to 75°)**
- 3½ **cups plus 1 tablespoon all-purpose flour, divided**
- 2 **teaspoons salt**
- 1 **tablespoon cornmeal or additional flour**

1. In a small bowl, dissolve yeast in water. In a large bowl, mix 3½ cups flour and salt. Using a rubber spatula, stir in yeast mixture to form a soft, sticky dough. Do not knead. Cover with plastic wrap; let rise at room temperature 1 hour.
2. Punch down dough. Turn onto a lightly floured surface; pat into a 9-in. square. Fold the square into thirds, forming a 9x3-in. rectangle. Fold rectangle into thirds, forming a 3-in. square. Turn dough over; place in a greased bowl. Cover with plastic wrap; let rise at room temperature until almost doubled, about 1 hour.
3. Punch down dough and repeat folding process. Return dough to bowl; refrigerate, covered, overnight.
4. Dust bottom of a disposable foil roasting pan with cornmeal. Turn dough onto a floured surface. Knead gently 6-8 times; shape into a 6-in. round loaf. Place in prepared pan; dust top of dough with remaining 1 tablespoon flour. Cover the pan with plastic wrap; let rise at room temperature until dough expands to a 7½-in. loaf, about 1¼ hours.
5. Preheat oven to 500°. Using a sharp knife, make a slash (¼ in. deep) across top of loaf. Cover pan tightly with foil. Bake on lowest oven rack 25 minutes.
6. Reduce oven setting to 450°. Remove foil; bake bread until deep golden brown, 25-30 minutes longer.

Remove loaf to a wire rack to cool.
FOR CHEDDAR CHEESE BREAD *Prepare dough as directed. After refrigerating dough overnight, knead in 4 ounces diced sharp cheddar cheese before shaping.*
FOR RUSTIC CRANBERRY & ORANGE BREAD *Prepare dough as directed. After refrigerating dough overnight, knead in 1 cup dried cranberries and 4 teaspoons grated orange peel before shaping.*
FOR GARLIC & OREGANO BREAD *Prepare dough as directed. After refrigerating dough overnight, microwave ½ cup peeled and quartered garlic cloves with ¼ cup 2% milk on high for 45 seconds. Drain garlic, discarding milk; knead garlic and 2 tablespoons minced fresh oregano into dough before shaping.*

FAST FIX
HERBED CHEESE STICKS

We love the breadsticks we get at our local pizza parlor when they're hot from the oven. Now I can make that same wonderful goodness at home.
—**HEATHER BATES** ATHENS, ME

START TO FINISH: 30 MIN.
MAKES: 16 CHEESE STICKS

- 1 **package (6½ ounces) pizza crust mix**
- 1½ **teaspoons garlic powder**
- 1 **tablespoon olive oil**
- 1 **cup shredded part-skim mozzarella cheese**
- ¼ **cup shredded Parmesan cheese**
- 1 **teaspoon Italian seasoning**
  Pizza sauce

1. Preheat oven to 450°. Mix the pizza dough according to package directions, adding garlic powder to dry mix. Cover; let rest 5 minutes.
2. Knead dough 4-5 times or until easy to handle. On a greased baking sheet, press dough into an 8-in. square. Brush top with oil; sprinkle with cheeses and Italian seasoning.
3. Bake 6-8 minutes or until cheese is lightly browned. Cut in half; cut each half crosswise into eight strips. Serve with pizza sauce.

THE ULTIMATE CHICKEN NOODLE SOUP
Gina Nistico
Milwaukee, WI

THE ULTIMATE CHICKEN NOODLE SOUP

My first Wisconsin winter was so cold, all I wanted to eat was soup. This recipe is in heavy rotation from November to April at our house.

—GINA NISTICO MILWAUKEE, WI

PREP: 15 MIN. • **COOK:** 45 MIN. + STANDING
MAKES: 10 SERVINGS (3½ QUARTS)

- 2½ **pounds bone-in chicken thighs**
- 1¼ **teaspoons pepper, divided**
- ½ **teaspoon salt**
- 1 **tablespoon canola oil**
- 1 **large onion, chopped**
- 1 **garlic clove, minced**
- 10 **cups chicken broth**
- 4 **celery ribs, chopped**
- 4 **medium carrots, chopped**
- 2 **bay leaves**
- 1 **teaspoon minced fresh thyme or ¼ teaspoon dried thyme**
- 3 **cups uncooked kluski or other egg noodles (about 8 ounces)**
- 1 **tablespoon chopped fresh parsley**
- 1 **tablespoon lemon juice**

1. Pat chicken dry with paper towels; sprinkle with ½ teaspoon pepper and salt. In a 6-qt. stockpot, heat oil over medium-high heat. Add chicken in batches, skin side down; cook until dark golden brown, 3-4 minutes. Remove chicken from pan; remove and discard skin. Discard drippings, reserving 2 tablespoons.

2. Add onion to the drippings; cook and stir over medium-high heat until tender, 4-5 minutes. Add garlic; cook 1 minute longer. Add broth, stirring to loosen browned bits from pan. Bring to a boil. Return chicken to pan. Add celery, carrots, bay leaves and thyme. Reduce heat; simmer, covered, until chicken is tender, 25-30 minutes.

3. Transfer the chicken to a plate. Remove soup from heat. Add noodles; let stand, covered, until noodles are tender, 20-22 minutes.

4. Meanwhile, when chicken is cool enough to handle, remove meat from bones; discard bones. Shred the meat into bite-size pieces. Return meat to stockpot. Stir in parsley and lemon juice. Adjust seasoning with salt and remaining ¾ teaspoon pepper. Remove bay leaves.

ROASTED BUTTERNUT SQUASH BREAD

Butternut squash is so versatile, I use it to make a sweet and savory bread perfect for breakfast, snacking or even dessert.
—**SARAH MEUSER** NEW MILFORD, CT

PREP: 40 MIN. • **BAKE:** 55 MIN. + COOLING
MAKES: 1 LOAF (16 SLICES)

- 3½ cups cubed peeled butternut squash (1-inch pieces)
- 2 tablespoons olive oil
- ½ cup butter, softened
- ½ cup sugar
- ½ cup packed brown sugar
- 2 large eggs
- 1 teaspoon vanilla extract
- 1½ cups whole wheat pastry flour
- 1 teaspoon baking soda
- 1 teaspoon ground cinnamon
- ¾ teaspoon salt
- ½ cup fat-free plain Greek yogurt
- ¼ teaspoon fine sea salt

1. Preheat oven to 375°. Place squash in a greased 15x10x1-in. baking pan. Drizzle with oil; toss to coat. Roast 25-30 minutes or until tender. Reduce oven setting to 325°.

2. Transfer squash to a large bowl; mash coarsely. In a large bowl, beat butter and sugars until blended. Add eggs, one at a time, beating well after each addition. Beat in the mashed squash and vanilla. In another bowl, whisk flour, baking soda, cinnamon and salt; add to the butter mixture alternately with yogurt, beating well after each addition.

3. Transfer to a greased 9x5-in. loaf pan; sprinkle with sea salt. Bake for 55-65 minutes or until a toothpick inserted in center comes out clean. Cool in pan 10 minutes before removing to a wire rack to cool.

CREAMY CHICKEN & BROCCOLI STEW

This recipe is so easy to make, but no one would ever guess. My husband, who doesn't like many chicken dishes, requests it regularly.
—**MARY WATKINS** LITTLE ELM, TX

PREP: 15 MIN. • **COOK:** 6 HOURS
MAKES: 8 SERVINGS

- 8 bone-in chicken thighs, skin removed (about 3 pounds)
- 1 cup Italian salad dressing
- ½ cup white wine or chicken broth
- 6 tablespoons butter, melted, divided
- 1 tablespoon dried minced onion
- 1 tablespoon garlic powder
- 1 tablespoon Italian seasoning
- ¾ teaspoon salt, divided
- ¾ teaspoon pepper, divided
- 1 can (10¾ ounces) condensed cream of mushroom soup, undiluted
- 1 package (8 ounces) cream cheese, softened
- 2 cups frozen broccoli florets, thawed
- 2 pounds red potatoes, quartered

1. Place chicken in a 4-qt. slow cooker. Combine the salad dressing, wine, 4 tablespoons butter, onion, garlic powder, Italian seasoning, ½ teaspoon salt and ½ teaspoon pepper in a small bowl; pour over chicken.

2. Cover and cook on low for 5 hours. Skim fat. Combine the soup, cream cheese and 2 cups of liquid from slow cooker in a small bowl until blended; add to slow cooker.

3. Cover and cook 45 minutes longer or until chicken is tender, adding the broccoli during the last 30 minutes of cooking.

4. Meanwhile, place potatoes in a large saucepan and cover with water. Bring to a boil. Reduce heat; cover and simmer until tender, 15-20 minutes. Drain and return to pan. Mash the potatoes with the remaining butter, salt and pepper. Serve with chicken and broccoli mixture.

ROASTED BUTTERNUT SQUASH BREAD

SOUR CREAM CUT-OUT BISCUITS

After trying countless ways to make biscuits and never being completely satisfied, I decided to use sour cream. Success! Split them while warm, spread on some butter and enjoy.

—**LORRAINE CALAND** SHUNIAH, ON

START TO FINISH: 30 MIN.
MAKES: 10 BISCUITS

- 2 **cups all-purpose flour**
- 2 **tablespoons sugar**
- 3 **teaspoons baking powder**
- ½ **teaspoon salt**
- ½ **teaspoon baking soda**
- 1 **cup (8 ounces) sour cream**
- 1 **tablespoon butter, melted**

1. Preheat oven to 425°. In a large bowl, whisk flour, sugar, baking powder, salt and baking soda. Stir in sour cream just until moistened.
2. Turn dough onto a lightly floured surface; knead gently 8-10 times. Pat or roll dough to ½-in. thickness; cut with a floured 2¼-in. biscuit cutter. Place 1 in. apart on an ungreased baking sheet. Bake until golden brown, 10-12 minutes. Brush biscuits with butter; serve warm.

GOES GREAT WITH

Make a mini meal when you pair up these biscuits and Merritt Heinrich's Pastrami Roll-Ups, page 105.

SOUR CREAM CUT-OUT BISCUITS

SPICED SWEET POTATO SOUP
Lisa Speer
Palm Beach, FL

CORNMEAL DINNER ROLLS

A robust sidekick to chili, soups and stews, these biscuits can also stand alone with a simple pat of butter and drizzle of honey.

—**BRYNN RADER** OLYMPIA, WA

PREP: 35 MIN. + RISING • **BAKE:** 15 MIN.
MAKES: 2½ DOZEN

- 2 **cups whole milk**
- ½ **cup sugar**
- ½ **cup butter, cubed**
- ⅓ **cup cornmeal**
- 1¼ **teaspoons salt**
- 1 **package (¼ ounce) active dry yeast**
- ¼ **cup warm water (110° to 115°)**
- 2 **large eggs**
- 4¾ to 5¾ **cups all-purpose flour**

TOPPING
- 2 **tablespoons butter, melted**
- 1 **tablespoon cornmeal**

1. In a large saucepan, combine the milk, sugar, butter, cornmeal and salt. Bring to a boil over medium heat, stirring constantly. Reduce heat; cook and stir until thickened, 5-8 minutes. Cool to 110°-115°.
2. In a small bowl, dissolve yeast in warm water. In a large bowl, combine the eggs, cornmeal mixture, yeast mixture and 2 cups flour; beat until smooth. Stir in enough remaining flour to form a soft dough (dough will be sticky).
3. Turn dough onto a floured surface; knead until smooth and elastic, about 6-8 minutes. Place in a greased bowl, turning once to grease the top. Cover with plastic wrap; let rise in a warm place until doubled, about 1 hour.
4. Punch dough down. Turn onto a lightly floured surface; divide into 30 balls. Place 2 in. apart on greased baking sheets. Cover with a clean kitchen towel; let rise in a warm place until doubled, about 45 minutes.
5. Uncover rolls; brush with melted butter and sprinkle with cornmeal. Bake at 375° until golden brown, 13-17 minutes. Remove from pans to wire racks; serve warm.

SLOW COOKER
SPICED SWEET POTATO SOUP

Sweet potatoes that simmer in a pot with ginger, cinnamon and curry make a cheerful soup that warms our spirits.

—**LISA SPEER** PALM BEACH, FL

PREP: 20 MIN. • **COOK:** 6 HOURS
MAKES: 12 SERVINGS (2¼ QUARTS)

- 2 **pounds sweet potatoes (about 4 medium), peeled and chopped**
- 1 **large sweet onion, finely chopped**
- 1 **medium sweet red pepper, finely chopped**
- 1½ **teaspoons curry powder**
- 1 **teaspoon sea salt**
- ½ **teaspoon ground cinnamon**
- ¼ **teaspoon ground ginger**
- ¼ **teaspoon ground allspice**
- ¼ **teaspoon grated lemon peel**
- ⅛ **teaspoon coarsely ground pepper**
- 6 **cups reduced-sodium chicken broth**
  Salted pumpkin seeds or pepitas, optional

1. In a 5-qt. slow cooker, combine the first 11 ingredients. Cook, covered, on low 6-8 hours or until the vegetables are tender.
2. Puree soup using an immersion blender. Or cool soup slightly and puree in batches in a blender; return to slow cooker and heat through. If desired, top each serving with pumpkin seeds.

COUSCOUS MEATBALL SOUP

This soup is great for a cold day. It's perfect with fresh crusty bread.
—JONATHAN PACE SAN FRANCISCO, CA

PREP: 25 MIN. • **COOK:** 40 MIN.
MAKES: 10 SERVINGS (2½ QUARTS)

- 1 pound lean ground beef (90% lean)
- 2 teaspoons dried basil
- 2 teaspoons dried oregano
- ½ teaspoon salt
- 1 large onion, finely chopped
- 2 teaspoons canola oil
- 1 bunch collard greens, chopped (8 cups)
- 1 bunch kale, chopped (8 cups)
- 2 cartons (32 ounces each) vegetable stock
- 1 tablespoon white wine vinegar
- ½ teaspoon crushed red pepper flakes
- ¼ teaspoon pepper
- 1 package (8.8 ounces) pearl (Israeli) couscous

1. In a small bowl, combine the beef, basil, oregano and salt. Shape into ½-in. balls. In a large nonstick skillet coated with cooking spray, brown meatballs; drain. Remove meatballs and set aside.

2. In the same skillet, brown onion in oil. Add greens and kale; cook 6-7 minutes longer or until wilted.

3. In a Dutch oven, combine greens mixture, meatballs, stock, vinegar, pepper flakes and pepper. Bring to a boil. Reduce heat; cover and simmer for 10 minutes. Return to a boil. Stir in couscous. Reduce heat; cover and simmer, stirring once, until couscous is tender, 10-15 minutes.

★ ★ ★ ★ ★ **READER REVIEW**

"Made this soup for dinner tonight and my 5- and 7-year-old boys loved it! It is a great way to sneak in some yummy, healthy greens."

DCRAVER TASTEOFHOME.COM

SESAME HERB PULL-APART BREAD

The beauty of this fresh herb bread is that I can make it a day ahead and pop it in the oven while completing a meal. It's great for soup dipping.
—MARY SHIVERS ADA, OK

PREP: 15 MIN. + CHILLING
BAKE: 30 MIN. + COOLING
MAKES: 24 SERVINGS

- 3 tablespoons minced fresh chives
- 3 tablespoons minced fresh parsley
- 1 teaspoon each dried basil, oregano and thyme
- 3 tablespoons sesame seeds
- 24 frozen bread dough dinner rolls
- ¼ cup butter, melted

1. In a bowl, mix chives and parsley. In another bowl, mix basil, oregano and thyme. In a greased 10-in. fluted tube pan, sprinkle 1 tablespoon sesame seeds, 2 tablespoons fresh herbs and 1 teaspoon dried herbs.

2. Arrange eight dinner rolls over herbs. Sprinkle with 1 tablespoon sesame seeds, 2 tablespoons of the fresh herbs and 1 teaspoon of the dried herbs. Drizzle with one-third of the butter. Repeat layers. Arrange the remaining rolls over top; drizzle with remaining butter. Refrigerate, covered, 12-24 hours.

3. Remove from the refrigerator 30 minutes before baking. Preheat oven to 350°. Bake rolls, uncovered, 20 minutes. Cover loosely with foil; bake rolls until golden brown, 10-15 minutes longer. Cool in pan 10 minutes before inverting onto a serving plate. Serve warm.

SEASAME HERB PULL-APART BREAD

CIOPPINO-STYLE SOUP

GARLIC BREAD MINI MUFFINS

Little garlic bread bites make a terrific addition to any buffet spread. We make sure to serve them warm.
—**KATHY YAROSH** APOPKA, FL

PREP: 25 MIN. • **BAKE:** 20 MIN.
MAKES: 2 DOZEN

- 6 ounces cream cheese, softened
- 1 teaspoon garlic powder
- 1 teaspoon onion powder
- ¾ cup shredded Colby-Monterey Jack cheese
- ¾ cup shredded Italian cheese blend
- 1 tube (11 ounces) refrigerated breadsticks
- 1 large egg, lightly beaten
- ½ cup shredded Parmesan cheese

1. Preheat oven to 375°. In a small bowl, beat cream cheese, garlic powder and onion powder until blended. In another bowl, toss Colby-Monterey Jack cheese with Italian cheese blend.
2. On a lightly floured surface, unroll breadstick dough; press perforations to seal. Roll dough to a 12x8-in. rectangle; cut the dough lengthwise in half.
3. Spread each 12x4-in. rectangle with half of the cream cheese mixture to within ¼-in. of edges. Sprinkle each with half of the combined cheeses; roll up jelly-roll style, starting with a long side. Pinch seam to seal. Cut rolls into 1-in. slices.
4. Place beaten egg and Parmesan cheese in separate shallow bowls. Dip a cut side of each slice in egg, then in Parmesan cheese; place in greased mini-muffin cups, cheese side up.
5. Bake until golden brown, 17-20 minutes. Serve warm.

TEST KITCHEN TIP
When a recipe calls for a lightly beaten egg, beat with a fork just until the yolk and white are combined.

CIOPPINO-STYLE SOUP

Try my healthy, flavorful soup for a light dinner. I make it for the family every New Year's Eve as a special meal. I like to include salmon along with the cod, shrimp and crab.
—**NANCY HEISHMAN** LAS VEGAS, NV

PREP: 20 MIN. • **COOK:** 1¼ HOURS
MAKES: 6 SERVINGS (2½ QUARTS)

- 2 tablespoons olive oil
- 2 medium red onions, chopped
- 3 garlic cloves, minced
- 1 can (28 ounces) no-salt-added crushed tomatoes
- 1 carton (32 ounces) vegetable stock
- 1 cup dry red wine
- 1½ teaspoons Italian seasoning
- ½ teaspoon pepper
- ½ teaspoon crushed red pepper flakes, optional
- 6 ounces uncooked shrimp (31–40 per pound), peeled and deveined
- 1 can (6 ounces) lump crabmeat, drained
- 2 cod fillets (6 ounces each), cut into 1-inch pieces
- ⅓ cup chopped fresh parsley
  Shredded Parmesan cheese, optional

1. In a 6-qt. stockpot, heat oil over medium heat. Add onions; cook and stir 4-6 minutes or until tender. Add garlic; cook 1 minute longer. Add the tomatoes, stock, wine, Italian seasoning and pepper; if desired, stir in pepper flakes. Bring to a boil. Reduce heat; simmer, covered, 1 hour to allow flavors to blend.
2. Add shrimp, crab, cod and parsley; cook until the shrimp turn pink and fish just begins to flake easily with a fork, 3-5 minutes longer. If desired, top each serving with cheese.

SPLIT PEA SOUP WITH HAM & JALAPENO

1.
Preheat oven to 350°. In a large bowl, combine muffin mixes and cayenne pepper. In another bowl, mix eggs, corn, buttermilk and ¼ cup oil until blended. Add to the dry ingredients; stir just until moistened. Fold in cheese, onion, chilies, pimientos and jalapeno.

2.
Brush remaining oil onto bottom of a 13x9-in. baking pan; place in oven 4-5 minutes or until hot. Pour batter into hot pan. Bake until edges are golden brown and a toothpick inserted in center comes out clean, 50-60 minutes. Cool in pan on a wire rack. Serve warm.

FAST FIX ▶

EASY CHEESY BISCUITS

I'm a big fan of homemade biscuits...but not the rolling and cutting that goes into making them. The drop biscuit method solves everything!

—**CHRISTINA ADDISON** BLANCHESTER, OH

START TO FINISH: 30 MIN.
MAKES: 1 DOZEN

- 3 **cups all-purpose flour**
- 3 **teaspoons baking powder**
- 1 **tablespoon sugar**
- 1 **teaspoon salt**
- ¾ **teaspoon cream of tartar**
- ½ **cup cold butter**
- 1 **cup shredded sharp cheddar cheese**
- 1 **garlic clove, minced**
- ¼ **to ½ teaspoon crushed red pepper flakes**
- 1¼ **cups 2% milk**

1. Preheat oven to 450°. In a large bowl, whisk flour, baking powder, sugar, salt and cream of tartar. Cut in butter until mixture resembles coarse crumbs. Stir in cheese, garlic and pepper flakes. Add milk; stir just until moistened.

2. Drop dough by heaping ¼ cupfuls 2 in. apart onto a greased baking sheet. Bake 18-20 minutes or until golden brown. Serve warm.

GOES GREAT WITH

Pick up a rotisserie chicken on the way home, then make these quick biscuits for a dinner that's ready in 30 minutes flat!

SLOW COOKER 🍲

SPLIT PEA SOUP WITH HAM & JALAPENO

To me, this spicy pea soup is my go-to cozy meal. I cook it low and slow all day, and it fills the house with a yummy aroma. It's so good with a crispy baguette.

—**CHELSEA TICHENOR**
HUNTINGTON BEACH, CA

PREP: 15 MIN. • **COOK:** 6 HOURS
MAKES: 6 SERVINGS (2¼ QUARTS)

- 2 **smoked ham hocks**
- 1 **package (16 ounces) dried green split peas**
- 4 **medium carrots, cut into ½-inch slices**
- 1 **medium onion, chopped**
- 1 **jalapeno pepper, seeded and minced**
- 3 **garlic cloves, minced**
- 8 **cups water**
- 1 **teaspoon salt**
- 1 **teaspoon pepper**

In a 4- or 5-qt. slow cooker, combine all ingredients. Cook, covered, on low until the meat is tender, 6-8 hours. Remove meat from bones when cool enough to handle; cut ham into small pieces and return to slow cooker.

NOTE *Wear disposable gloves when cutting hot peppers; the oils can burn skin. Avoid touching your face.*

CONFETTI CORN BREAD

My grandmother Virginia always served a Southwest-inspired cornbread. To honor her, I made a recipe that cuts down on the chopping but never skimps on flavor.

—**ANGIE PRICE** BRADFORD, TN

PREP: 20 MIN. • **BAKE:** 50 MIN.
MAKES: 12 SERVINGS

- 2 **packages (8½ ounces each) corn bread/muffin mix**
- ¼ **teaspoon cayenne pepper**
- 2 **large eggs**
- 1 **can (14¾ ounces) cream-style corn**
- ½ **cup buttermilk**
- ¼ **cup plus 1½ teaspoons canola oil, divided**
- 1 **cup shredded cheddar cheese**
- 1 **small onion, chopped**
- 1 **can (4 ounces) chopped green chilies**
- 1 **jar (2 ounces) pimiento strips, drained**
- 1 **jalapeno pepper, seeded and chopped**

**EASY CHEESY
BISCUITS**

OLIVE & ONION QUICK BREAD

I've been baking for over 50 years and never tire of trying new recipes for my family, friends and co-workers. Baking actually relaxes me. I feel like an artist creating a masterpiece.
—**PAULA MARCHESI** LENHARTSVILLE, PA

PREP: 15 MIN. • **BAKE:** 45 MIN. + COOLING
MAKES: 1 LOAF (12 SLICES)

- 1 tablespoon canola oil
- 1 medium onion, finely chopped
- 2 cups all-purpose flour
- 1 tablespoon minced fresh rosemary
- 1 teaspoon baking soda
- ½ teaspoon salt
- 2 large eggs
- 1 cup buttermilk
- 2 tablespoons butter, melted
- ¼ cup plus 2 tablespoons sharp cheddar cheese, divided
- ¼ cup each chopped pitted green and ripe olives

1. Preheat oven to 350°. In a skillet, heat oil over medium-high heat. Add the onion; cook and stir until tender, 2-3 minutes. Remove from heat.
2. In a large bowl, whisk flour, rosemary, baking soda and salt. In another bowl, whisk eggs, buttermilk and melted butter until blended. Add to the flour mixture; stir just until moistened. Fold in ¼ cup cheese, olives and onion.
3. Transfer to a greased 8x4-in. loaf pan. Bake 40 minutes. Sprinkle remaining cheese over top. Bake until a toothpick inserted in center comes out clean, 5-10 minutes longer. Cool in pan 10 minutes before removing to a wire rack to cool.

HONEY-SQUASH DINNER ROLLS

HONEY-SQUASH DINNER ROLLS

These puffy dinner rolls take on rich color when you add squash to the dough. Any squash variety works, and I've even used cooked carrots with success.
—**MARCIA WHITNEY** GAINESVILLE, FL

PREP: 40 MIN. + RISING • **BAKE:** 20 MIN.
MAKES: 2 DOZEN

- 2 packages (¼ ounce each) active dry yeast
- 2 teaspoons salt
- ¼ teaspoon ground nutmeg
- 6 to 6½ cups all-purpose flour
- 1¼ cups 2% milk
- ½ cup butter, cubed
- ½ cup honey
- 1 package (12 ounces) frozen mashed winter squash, thawed (about 1⅓ cups)
- 1 large egg, lightly beaten
  Poppy seeds, salted pumpkin seeds or pepitas, or sesame seeds

1. In a large bowl, mix yeast, salt, nutmeg and 3 cups flour. In a small saucepan, heat milk, butter and honey to 120°-130°. Add to dry ingredients; beat on medium speed 2 minutes. Add squash; beat on high 2 minutes. Stir in enough remaining flour to form a soft dough (dough will be sticky).
2. Turn the dough onto a floured surface; knead until smooth and elastic, 6-8 minutes. Place in a greased bowl, turning once to grease the top. Cover dough with plastic wrap and let rise in a warm place until doubled, about 1 hour.
3. Punch down dough. Turn onto a lightly floured surface; divide and shape into 24 balls. Divide between two greased 9-in. round baking pans. Cover with kitchen towels; let rise in a warm place until doubled, about 45 minutes.
4. Preheat oven to 375°. Brush tops with beaten egg; sprinkle with seeds. Bake rolls until dark golden brown, 20-25 minutes. Cover loosely with foil during the last 5-7 minutes if needed to prevent overbrowning. Remove from pans to wire racks; serve warm.

ITALIAN SAUSAGE
& KALE SOUP

SLOW COOKER 🍲

ITALIAN SAUSAGE & KALE SOUP

The first time I made this colorful soup, our home smelled absolutely amazing. We knew it was a keeper to see us through cold winter days.

—SARAH STOMBAUGH CHICAGO, IL

PREP: 20 MIN. • **COOK:** 8 HOURS
MAKES: 8 SERVINGS (3½ QUARTS)

- 1 pound bulk hot Italian sausage
- 6 cups chopped fresh kale
- 2 cans (15½ ounces each) great northern beans, rinsed and drained
- 1 can (28 ounces) crushed tomatoes
- 4 large carrots, finely chopped (about 3 cups)
- 1 medium onion, chopped
- 3 garlic cloves, minced
- 1 teaspoon dried oregano
- ¼ teaspoon salt
- ⅛ teaspoon pepper
- 5 cups chicken stock
  Grated Parmesan cheese

1. In a large skillet, cook sausage over medium heat 6-8 minutes or until no longer pink, breaking into crumbles; drain. Transfer to a 5-qt. slow cooker.
2. Add kale, beans, tomatoes, carrots, onion, garlic, seasonings and stock to slow cooker. Cook, covered, on low 8-10 hours or until vegetables are tender. Top each serving with cheese.

★ ★ ★ ★ ★ **READER REVIEW**

"This was the perfect combination of soup, stew and chili. I only added about half the kale, but it was still very prominent in the recipe."

REMENEC TASTEOFHOME.COM

CHICKEN & BEAN CHILI

Whatever the season, it can be chili time whenever you want to please a hungry crowd. This creamy chicken chili is a must at my soup party every year.

—THERESA BAEHR TRAVERSE CITY, MI

PREP: 25 MIN. • **COOK:** 15 MIN.
MAKES: 10 SERVINGS (2¾ QUARTS)

- 1 tablespoon olive oil
- 1 tablespoon butter
- 1 medium onion, finely chopped
- 2 large garlic cloves, minced
- 2 cans (16 ounces each) kidney beans, rinsed and drained
- 2 cans (15 ounces each) pinto beans, rinsed and drained
- 1 can (28 ounces) diced tomatoes, undrained
- 3 cups shredded cooked chicken
- 1⅔ cups whole milk
- 1 cup beer or reduced-sodium chicken broth
- 2 tablespoons chicken bouillon granules
- 1 tablespoon sugar
- 1 bay leaf
- 2 teaspoons ground cumin
- 1 teaspoon each onion powder, garlic powder and chili powder
- ½ teaspoon salt
- ¼ teaspoon crushed red pepper flakes
- ¼ teaspoon ground celery seed
- ¼ teaspoon pepper
- ⅛ teaspoon ground turmeric

1. In a Dutch oven, heat the oil and butter over medium-high heat. Add onion; cook and stir 5-7 minutes or until tender. Add the garlic; cook 1 minute longer.
2. Stir in remaining ingredients; bring to a boil, stirring occasionally. Reduce the heat; simmer, uncovered, 5 minutes. Remove bay leaf.

TEST KITCHEN TIP
Save some money by buying bay leaves in bulk at the grocery store—you can store them long-term in your freezer!

ANDOUILLE SAUSAGE SOUP

I wanted a vegetable-filled soup with a lot of flavor. Adding andouille sausage made this recipe spicy enough that even my sons enjoy eating it!

—STEVEN THURNER JANESVILLE, WI

PREP: 20 MIN. • **COOK:** 35 MIN.
MAKES: 10 SERVINGS (3½ QUARTS)

- 1 tablespoon canola oil
- 2 large onions, chopped
- 3 medium carrots, chopped
- 1 medium green pepper, chopped
- 2 garlic cloves, minced
- 1 package (12 ounces) fully cooked andouille chicken sausage links, cut into ¼-inch slices
- 1½ pounds red potatoes (about 5 medium), cut into ½-inch cubes
- 1 can (28 ounces) crushed tomatoes in puree
- 1 teaspoon Worcestershire sauce
- ¼ teaspoon pepper
- 1 carton (32 ounces) reduced-sodium beef broth
- 2 teaspoons liquid smoke, optional
- ¼ teaspoon cayenne pepper, optional
  Sour cream, optional

1. In a 6-qt. stockpot, heat oil over medium heat. Add onions, carrots and green pepper; cook and stir 8-10 minutes or until tender. Add garlic; cook 1 minute longer. Remove from the pot.
2. In the same pot, brown sausage over medium heat. Add potatoes, tomatoes, Worcestershire sauce, pepper, broth and onion mixture. If desired, stir in liquid smoke and cayenne. Bring to a boil. Reduce heat; simmer, covered, 15-20 minutes or until potatoes are tender. If desired, top servings with sour cream.

ANDOUILLE SAUSAGE SOUP
Steven Thurner
Janesville, WI

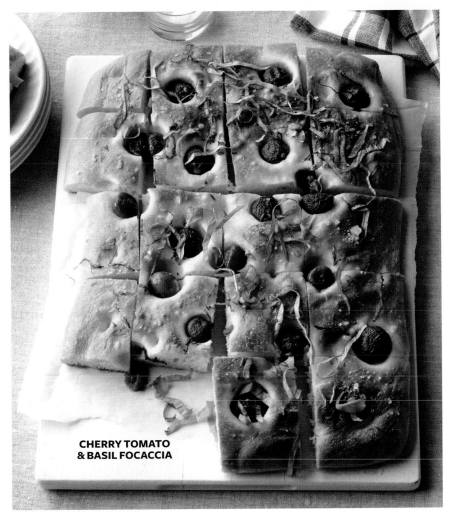

CHERRY TOMATO & BASIL FOCACCIA

CHERRY TOMATO & BASIL FOCACCIA

When I had 80 pounds of tomatoes, I got creative incorporating them into meals. Sometimes I slice this loaf into squares to make sandwiches with fresh mozzarella cheese and deli meats.

—**KATIE FERRIER** HOUSTON, TX

PREP: 45 MIN. + RISING • **BAKE:** 15 MIN.
MAKES: 24 SERVINGS

- 1 **package (¼ ounce) active dry yeast**
- 2 **cups warm 2% milk (110° to 115°)**
- ¼ **cup canola oil**
- 4½ **teaspoons sugar**
- 1 **teaspoon salt**
- 5 **to 5½ cups all-purpose flour**
- 2 **cups cherry tomatoes**
- ⅓ **cup olive oil**
- 2 **tablespoons cornmeal**
- 3 **tablespoons thinly sliced fresh basil**
- 1 **teaspoon coarse salt**
- ⅛ **teaspoon pepper**

1. In a small bowl, dissolve yeast in warm milk. In a large bowl, combine canola oil, sugar, salt, yeast mixture and 2 cups flour; beat on medium speed until smooth. Stir in enough remaining flour to form a stiff dough (dough will be sticky).

2. Turn dough onto a floured surface; knead until smooth and elastic, about 6-8 minutes. Place in a greased bowl, turning once to grease the top. Cover with plastic wrap and let rise in a warm place until doubled, about 45 minutes.

3. Meanwhile, fill a large saucepan two-thirds with water; bring to a boil. Cut a shallow "X" on the bottom of each tomato. Using a slotted spoon, place tomatoes, a cup at a time, in boiling water for 30 seconds or just until skin at the "X" begins to loosen.

4. Remove the tomatoes and drop immediately into ice water. Pull off and discard skins. Place tomatoes in a small bowl; drizzle with oil.

5. Preheat oven to 425°. Sprinkle two greased baking sheets with cornmeal; set aside. Punch down dough. Turn onto a lightly floured surface. Cover dough with a clean kitchen towel; let rest 10 minutes. Divide dough in half. Shape each into a 12x8-in. rectangle and place on prepared baking sheets.

6. Using fingertips, press several dimples into dough. Pour tomato mixture over dough; sprinkle with basil, coarse salt and pepper. Let rise in a warm place until doubled, about 30 minutes.

7. Bake until golden brown, 15-18 minutes.

CHEESE-FILLED GARLIC ROLLS

To change up plain old dinner rolls, I added mozzarella. Now my family wants them at every gathering. I don't mind!

—**ROSALIE FITTERY** PHILADELPHIA, PA

PREP: 20 MIN. + RISING • **BAKE:** 15 MIN.
MAKES: 2 DOZEN

- 1 **loaf (1 pound) frozen bread dough, thawed**
- 24 **cubes part-skim mozzarella cheese (¾ inch each), about 10 ounces**
- 3 **tablespoons butter, melted**
- 2 **teaspoons minced fresh parsley**
- 1 **garlic clove, minced**
- ½ **teaspoon Italian seasoning**
- ½ **teaspoon crushed red pepper flakes**
- 2 **tablespoons grated Parmigiano-Reggiano cheese**

1. Divide dough into 24 portions. Shape each portion around a cheese cube to cover completely; pinch to seal. Place each roll in a greased muffin cup, seam side down. Cover with kitchen towels; let rise in a warm place until doubled, about 30 minutes. Preheat oven to 350°.

2. In a small bowl, mix butter, parsley, garlic, Italian seasoning and pepper flakes. Brush over rolls; sprinkle with cheese. Bake until golden brown, 15-18 minutes.

3. Cool 5 minutes before removing from pans. Serve warm.

Sweet Treats

Family time doesn't have to end just because the main meal is over! Everyone will hang tight at the table when dessert's on the menu, and we have just the recipes to wow.

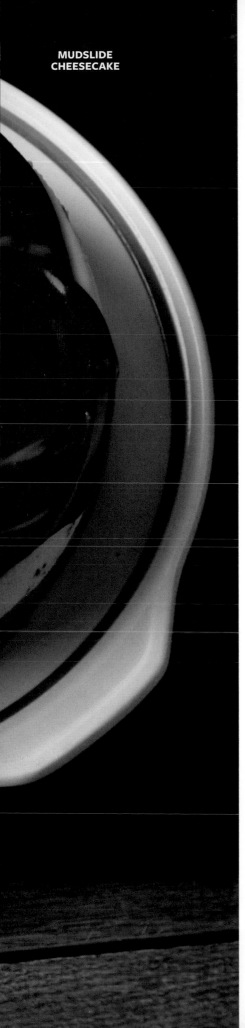

MUDSLIDE CHEESECAKE

Change up cheesecakes with different liqueur flavorings. This mudslide version with coffee and Irish cream is my husband's personal favorite.

—SUE GRONHOLZ BEAVER DAM, WI

PREP: 30 MIN. • **BAKE:** 60 MIN. + COOLING
MAKES: 16 SERVINGS

- 1 cup chocolate wafer crumbs
- 3 tablespoons sugar
- 2 tablespoons butter, melted

FILLING
- 1 cup (6 ounces) semisweet chocolate chips
- 4 packages (8 ounces each) cream cheese, softened
- 1½ cups sugar
- 4 tablespoons all-purpose flour
- 4 large eggs, room temperature
- 2 teaspoons vanilla extract
- 2 tablespoons coffee liqueur
- ¾ cup Irish cream liqueur

GANACHE
- ½ cup (3 ounces) semisweet chocolate chips
- ¼ cup heavy whipping cream

1. Preheat oven to 325°. Wrap a double thickness of heavy-duty foil (about 18 in. square) around a greased 9-in. springform pan. Mix cookie crumbs and sugar; stir in butter. Press onto bottom of prepared pan.

2. To prepare filling, microwave the chocolate chips on high until melted, about 1 minute. Beat cream cheese and sugar until smooth. Add flour; mix well. Add eggs and vanilla; beat on low just until blended. Measure out 2 cups batter, and stir in the coffee liqueur; add melted chocolate chips and stir until blended. Pour over crust. Add Irish cream liqueur to remaining batter; spoon over chocolate layer. Place springform pan in a larger baking pan; add 1 in. of hot water to larger pan.

3. Bake until center is just set and top appears dull, 60-75 minutes. Remove springform pan from water bath. Cool cheesecake on a wire rack 10 minutes. Loosen sides from pan with a knife; remove the foil. Cool 1 hour longer. Refrigerate overnight, covering when completely cooled.

4. For ganache, microwave chocolate chips and whipping cream on high until chips melt; cool slightly. Remove rim from pan; spread ganache on chilled cheesecake.

CRANBERRY PECAN OATMEAL COOKIES

I needed a new cookie, so I tweaked an old 4-H recipe. This updated oatmeal cookie with cranberries and nuts is a real winner in my house.

—TAMMY HOGGATT OMAHA, NE

PREP: 25 MIN. • **BAKE:** 15 MIN./BATCH
MAKES: ABOUT 5 DOZEN

- ½ cup butter, softened
- ½ cup sugar
- ½ cup packed brown sugar
- 1 large egg
- ½ teaspoon vanilla extract
- 1 cup all-purpose flour
- ¾ teaspoon ground cinnamon
- ½ teaspoon salt
- ½ teaspoon baking powder
- ½ teaspoon baking soda
- 1½ cups old-fashioned or quick-cooking oats
- 1 cup dried cranberries, coarsely chopped
- 1 cup chopped pecans

1. Preheat oven to 350°. Cream butter and sugars until light and fluffy; beat in egg and vanilla. In another bowl, whisk together flour, cinnamon, salt, baking powder and baking soda; gradually beat into creamed mixture. Stir in remaining ingredients.

2. Drop by tablespoonfuls 1 in. apart onto ungreased baking sheets. Bake until light golden brown, 12-15 minutes. Cool on pans 2 minutes. Remove to wire racks to cool.

TEST KITCHEN TIP
Wondering if your baking powder and baking soda are still good? Here's an easy test: For baking powder, place 1 teaspoon baking powder in a cup and add ⅓ cup hot tap water. For baking soda, place ¼ teaspoon baking soda in a cup and add 2 teaspoons vinegar. If active bubbling occurs, the products are fine to use. If not, toss 'em.

**EASY
LEMON PIE**

EASY LEMON PIE

I've had this one-bowl lemon pie recipe for years. It's my twist on chocolate French silk pie, and it's easy to do with refrigerated pie pastry.
—GLENNA TOOMAN BOISE, ID

PREP: 15 MIN. • **BAKE:** 40 MIN. + CHILLING
MAKES: 8 SERVINGS

- 1 **sheet refrigerated pie pastry**
- ½ **cup sugar**
- 2 **tablespoons all-purpose flour**
- 4 **large eggs**
- 1 **cup light corn syrup**
- 1 **teaspoon grated lemon peel**
- ⅓ **cup lemon juice**
- 2 **tablespoons butter, melted**

WHIPPED CREAM

- 1 **cup heavy whipping cream**
- 2 **tablespoons confectioners' sugar**

1. Preheat oven to 350°. Unroll pastry sheet into a 9-in. pie plate; flute edge. Refrigerate while preparing filling.
2. In a bowl, mix sugar and flour until blended. Whisk in eggs, corn syrup, lemon peel, lemon juice and melted butter until blended. Pour into the pastry-lined pie plate.
3. Bake on a lower oven rack until filling is golden brown and thickened, 40-45 minutes; cover edge loosely with foil during last 15 minutes if needed to prevent overbrowning. Remove foil; cool 1 hour on a wire rack. Refrigerate, covered, 2 hours or until cold.
4. For whipped cream, in a bowl, beat cream until it begins to thicken. Add the confectioners' sugar; beat until soft peaks form. Serve the pie with whipped cream.

TRUFFLE-FILLED COOKIE TARTS

I made chocolate truffles as a Christmas tradition for many years. I created this recipe to incorporate my truffles into the center of fudgy cookies. It was a hit with friends and family.
—PATRICIA HARMON BADEN, PA

PREP: 65 MIN. + COOLING
COOK: 20 MIN. + CHILLING
MAKES: 2½ DOZEN

- ½ **cup butter, softened**
- ½ **cup sugar**
- ½ **cup packed brown sugar**
- 1 **large egg**
- 1 **teaspoon vanilla extract**
- 1½ **cups all-purpose flour**
- ⅓ **cup baking cocoa**
- ¼ **teaspoon baking soda**

FILLING

- 2 **cups (12 ounces) semisweet chocolate chips**
- ⅔ **cup heavy whipping cream**
- ¼ **cup butter, cubed**
- 2 **large egg yolks**
  Chocolate sprinkles

1. Preheat oven to 400°. In a large bowl, beat butter and sugars until blended. Beat in egg and vanilla. In another bowl, whisk flour, cocoa and baking soda; gradually beat into creamed mixture.
2. Shape level tablespoons of dough into 2½-in.-wide patties. Press onto bottoms and up the sides of greased mini-muffin cups.
3. Bake until set, 8-10 minutes. Immediately press a deep indentation in center of each with the end of a wooden spoon handle. Cool in pans 5 minutes. Remove to wire racks to cool completely.
4. For the filling, in a small heavy saucepan, combine chocolate chips, cream and butter; cook and stir over medium heat until smooth. Remove from heat.
5. In a small bowl, whisk a small amount of hot mixture into egg yolks; return all to pan, whisking constantly. Cook, stirring constantly, over low heat until mixture is thickened and a thermometer reads at least 160°, 15-17 minutes. Do not allow to boil. Immediately transfer filling to a bowl; cool 20 minutes, stirring occasionally.
6. Spoon 1 tablespoon filling into each crust. Top with sprinkles. Refrigerate until cold, about 1 hour.

GOES GREAT WITH

Serve these rich cookie tarts after a light dinner. They're the perfect decadent follow-up to salad or sandwiches!

**TRUFFLE-FILLED
COOKIE TARTS**

CHAI TEA
SANDWICH COOKIES
Lauren Knoelke
Milwaukee, WI

CHAI TEA SANDWICH COOKIES

You'll love these cookies filled with a dreamy chai-infused ganache. They're great as a simple dessert after a meal, with a cup of tea, as a breakfast treat—or anytime at all.

—LAUREN KNOELKE MILWAUKEE, WI

PREP: 45 MIN. + CHILLING
BAKE: 10 MIN./BATCH + COOLING
MAKES: ABOUT 3½ DOZEN

- 8 ounces white baking chocolate, finely chopped
- ⅓ cup heavy whipping cream
- 2 chai-flavored black tea bags

COOKIES

- 2 cups all-purpose flour
- ½ cup sugar
- ½ teaspoon ground cinnamon
- ½ teaspoon ground cardamom
- ⅛ teaspoon salt
- ⅛ teaspoon pepper
- 1 cup cold butter, cut into 16 pieces
- 2 teaspoons vanilla extract

1. For ganache, place chocolate in a small bowl. In a small saucepan, bring cream just to a boil; remove from heat. Add tea bags; let stand 10 minutes. Discard tea bags.

2. Reheat the cream just to a boil. Pour over the chocolate; let stand 5 minutes. Stir with a whisk until smooth. Cool to room temperature, stirring occasionally, until ganache thickens to a spreading consistency, about 1 hour.

3. Meanwhile, in a large bowl, whisk flour, sugar, cinnamon, cardamom, salt and pepper; cut in butter with vanilla until crumbly. Knead until dough holds together when pressed. Shape into two disks; wrap each in plastic wrap. Refrigerate 15 minutes or until firm enough to roll.

4. Preheat oven to 350°. On a lightly floured surface, gently roll dough to ⅛-in. thickness, lifting and rotating dough as needed. Cut with a 1½-in. round cookie cutter. Place 1 in. apart on ungreased baking sheets. Bake until light brown, 10-12 minutes. Remove from pans to wire racks to cool completely.

5. Spread 1 heaping teaspoon ganache on bottoms of half of cookies; cover with remaining cookies. Let stand until set.

FREEZE OPTION *Prepare the dough. Transfer wrapped disks to a resealable plastic freezer bag; freeze. To use, thaw dough in refrigerator until soft enough to roll. Make ganache. Prepare, bake and fill cookies as directed.*

CHOCOLATE S'MORES TART

I created this tart for my kids, who love having s'mores on the fire pit. It's truly indulgent. We simply can't get enough of the billowy marshmallow topping.
—DINA CROWELL FREDERICKSBURG, VA

PREP: 55 MIN. + CHILLING
MAKES: 16 SERVINGS

1½ cups graham cracker crumbs
¼ cup sugar
⅓ cup butter, melted
FILLING
10 ounces bittersweet chocolate, chopped
¼ cup butter, cubed
1½ cups heavy whipping cream
TOPPING
5 large egg whites
1 cup sugar
¼ teaspoon cream of tartar

1. In a small bowl, mix the cracker crumbs and sugar; stir in the butter. Press onto bottom and ½ in. up sides of an ungreased 9-in. fluted tart pan with removable bottom. Refrigerate 30 minutes.

2. Place chocolate and butter in a large bowl. In a small saucepan, bring cream just to a boil. Pour over the chocolate and butter; let stand 5 minutes. Stir with a whisk until smooth. Pour into prepared tart shell. Refrigerate 1 hour or until set. Place egg whites in a large bowl; let stand at room temperature 30 minutes.

3. In top of a double boiler or a metal bowl over simmering water, combine egg whites, sugar and cream of tartar. Beat on low speed 1 minute. Continue beating on low until a thermometer reads 160°, about 5 minutes. Transfer to a large bowl; beat on high until stiff glossy peaks form and the mixture is slightly cooled, about 5 minutes.

4. Spread meringue over tart. If desired, heat meringue with a kitchen torch or broil 2 in. from heat until meringue is lightly browned, 30-45 seconds. Refrigerate leftovers.
NOTE *For a firmer crust, bake at 350° until the crust is lightly browned, 10-12 minutes. Cool on a wire rack.*

CHOCOLATE S'MORES TART

NEW YORK-STYLE CHEESECAKE MOUSSE

This cheesecake mousse actually tastes better after chilling overnight. Once chilled, it can be covered with plastic wrap and refrigerated for up to three days. Berries are optional, but they're a flavorful way to dress up this dessert.
—CAROLINE WAMELINK
CLEVELAND HEIGHTS, OH

PREP: 20 MIN. + CHILLING
MAKES: 12 SERVINGS

1 package (8 ounces) cream cheese, softened
½ cup confectioners' sugar
1½ teaspoons vanilla extract
½ teaspoon grated lemon peel
¾ cup heavy whipping cream, whipped
½ cup graham cracker crumbs
4 teaspoons sugar
2 tablespoons butter, melted
Sliced fresh strawberries, optional

1. In a large bowl, beat cream cheese, confectioners' sugar, vanilla and lemon peel until fluffy. Fold in the whipped cream. Divide among 12 dessert dishes. Cover and refrigerate at least 2 hours.

2. Meanwhile, preheat oven to 375°. Combine the cracker crumbs and sugar in a small bowl; add the butter and mix well. Press to a ¼-in. thickness on an ungreased baking sheet. Bake until lightly browned, 10-12 minutes. Cool completely.

3. Just before serving, crumble graham cracker mixture; sprinkle over mousse. Top with strawberries if desired.

★ ★ ★ ★ ★ **READER REVIEW**
"These were delicious! I used frozen sliced strawberries in sugar syrup, as strawberries were not in season here, and the juice from the syrup blended beautifully."
DONNANJ TASTEOFHOME.COM

EASY FOUR-LAYER CHOCOLATE DESSERT

I grew up on these nutty, chocolaty layered treats. Now I make them for both my mom and myself, since I know she loves them, too.

—KRISTEN STECKLEIN WAUKESHA, WI

PREP: 25 MIN. • **BAKE:** 15 MIN. + COOLING
MAKES: 15 SERVINGS

- 1   cup all-purpose flour
- ½   cup cold butter
- 1   cup chopped walnuts, toasted, divided
- 1   package (8 ounces) cream cheese, softened
- 1   cup confectioners' sugar
- 2   cartons (8 ounces each) frozen whipped topping, thawed, divided
- 2½ cups 2% milk
- 2   packages (3.9 ounces each) instant chocolate pudding mix
- 1   cup semisweet chocolate chunks
     Chocolate syrup

1. Preheat oven to 350°. Place the flour in a small bowl; cut in butter until crumbly. Stir in ½ cup walnuts. Press onto bottom of an ungreased 13x9-in. baking dish. Bake until light golden brown, 12-15 minutes. Cool completely on a wire rack.
2. In a small bowl, beat the cream cheese and confectioners' sugar until smooth; fold in one carton whipped topping. Spread over the crust. In a large bowl, whisk milk and pudding mix 2 minutes. Gently spread over cream cheese layer. Top with the remaining whipped topping. Sprinkle with chocolate chunks and remaining walnuts. Refrigerate until cold.
3. Cut into bars. Just before serving, drizzle with chocolate syrup.
NOTE *To toast nuts, bake in a shallow pan in a 350° oven for 5-10 minutes or cook in a skillet over low heat, stirring occasionally, until lightly browned.*

LEMON SLICE
SUGAR COOKIES

LEMON SLICE SUGAR COOKIES

Here's a refreshing variation of my grandmother's sugar cookie recipe. Lemon pudding mix and icing add a subtle tartness that tingles your taste buds.

—MELISSA TURKINGTON CAMANO ISLAND, WA

PREP: 15 MIN. + CHILLING
BAKE: 10 MIN. + COOLING
MAKES: 2 DOZEN

- ½   cup unsalted butter, softened
- 1   package (3.4 ounces) instant lemon pudding mix
- ½   cup sugar
- 1   large egg
- 2   tablespoons 2% milk
- 1½ cups all-purpose flour
- 1   teaspoon baking powder
- ¼   teaspoon salt
ICING
- ⅔   cup confectioners' sugar
- 2   to 4 teaspoons lemon juice

1. In a large bowl, cream butter, pudding mix and sugar until light and fluffy. Beat in the egg and milk. In another bowl, whisk flour, baking powder and salt; gradually beat into creamed mixture.
2. Divide the dough in half. On a lightly floured surface, shape each into a 6-in.-long roll. Wrap in plastic wrap; refrigerate 3 hours or until firm.
3. Preheat oven to 375°. Unwrap and cut the dough crosswise into ½-in. slices. Place 1 in. apart on ungreased baking sheets. Bake until edges are light brown, 8-10 minutes. Cool on pans 2 minutes. Remove to wire racks to cool completely.
4. In a small bowl, mix confectioners' sugar and enough lemon juice to reach a drizzling consistency. Drizzle over cookies. Let stand until set.
TO MAKE AHEAD *Dough can be made 2 days in advance. Wrap in plastic wrap and place in a resealable bag. Store in the refrigerator.*
FREEZE OPTION *Place wrapped logs in a resealable plastic freezer bag and freeze. To use, unwrap frozen logs and cut into slices. Bake as directed, increasing time by 1-2 minutes.*

BERRY & GANACHE CHEESECAKE BARS

I use fresh raspberries with chocolate ganache to make cheesecake bars that dare you to walk away empty-handed.

—**CARMELL CHILDS** FERRON, UT

PREP: 35 MIN. • **BAKE:** 25 MIN. + CHILLING
MAKES: 2 DOZEN

- 1½ cups graham cracker crumbs
- ¼ cup finely chopped pecans
- ¼ teaspoon salt
- ¼ cup butter, melted

CHEESECAKE LAYER
- 2 packages (8 ounces each) cream cheese, softened
- ½ cup sugar
- ½ teaspoon vanilla extract
- 2 large eggs, lightly beaten

TOPPING
- 1½ cups (9 ounces) semisweet chocolate chips
- 1 cup heavy whipping cream
- 2 tablespoons balsamic vinegar
- 1 tablespoon light corn syrup
- 1½ cups fresh raspberries or blueberries

1. Preheat oven to 350°. In a bowl, mix cracker crumbs, pecans and salt; stir in melted butter. Press onto bottom of a greased 13x9-in. baking pan. Bake until lightly browned, 8-10 minutes. Cool on a wire rack.

2. In a large bowl, beat cream cheese and sugar until smooth. Beat in vanilla. Add eggs; beat on low speed just until blended. Spread over crust. Bake until center is almost set, 15-20 minutes. Cool 1 hour on a wire rack.

3. Place chocolate chips in a small bowl. In a saucepan, bring cream just to a boil. Pour over the chocolate; let stand 5 minutes. Stir with a whisk until smooth. Stir in the vinegar and corn syrup; cool slightly, stirring occasionally. Pour over cheesecake layer; let stand 5 minutes. Top with the berries.

4. Refrigerate at least 3 hours, covering when completely cooled. Cut into bars.

BERRY & GANACHE CHEESECAKE BARS

CHOCOLATE-RASPBERRY WHOOPIE PIES

I've saved this jam-filled whoopie pie recipe for years after cutting it out of a newspaper. It's one of my grandson's personal favorites.
—**NANCY FOUST** STONEBORO, PA

PREP: 40 MIN.
BAKE: 10 MIN./BATCH + COOLING
MAKES: ABOUT 2½ DOZEN

- ½ cup butter, softened
- 1 cup sugar
- 1 large egg
- 1 teaspoon vanilla extract
- 2 cups all-purpose flour
- ½ cup baking cocoa
- 1½ teaspoons baking soda
- ½ teaspoon baking powder
- ½ teaspoon salt
- 1 cup 2% milk

FILLING
- 1 jar (7 ounces) marshmallow creme
- ½ cup shortening
- ⅓ cup seedless raspberry jam
- 1 teaspoon vanilla extract
- 2 cups confectioners' sugar

1. Preheat oven to 400°. In a large bowl, cream butter and sugar until light and fluffy. Beat in egg and vanilla. In another bowl, whisk flour, cocoa, baking soda, baking powder and salt; add to creamed mixture alternately with milk, beating well after each addition.

2. Drop dough by tablespoonfuls 2 in. apart onto greased baking sheets. Bake until set and tops spring back when lightly touched, 6-8 minutes. Remove from pans to wire racks to cool completely.

3. For filling, in a large bowl, beat marshmallow creme and shortening until blended. Beat in jam and vanilla. Gradually beat in confectioners' sugar until smooth. Spread on bottoms of half of the cookies; cover with the remaining cookies.

BLUEBERRY, BASIL & GOAT CHEESE PIE

BLUEBERRY, BASIL & GOAT CHEESE PIE

To send off a friend who was moving away, I made a galette of blueberries, creamy goat cheese and fresh basil. Bake one, share, and start a precious memory.
—**ASHLEY LECKER** GREEN BAY, WI

PREP: 15 MIN. • **BAKE:** 40 MIN. + COOLING
MAKES: 6 SERVINGS

- Pastry for single-crust pie (9 inches)
- 2 cups fresh blueberries
- 2 tablespoons plus 2 teaspoons sugar, divided
- 1 tablespoon cornstarch
- 1 tablespoon minced fresh basil
- 1 large egg
- 1 teaspoon water
- ¼ cup crumbled goat cheese
- Fresh basil leaves, torn

1. Preheat oven to 375°. On a floured sheet of parchment paper, roll pastry into a 10-in. circle. Transfer to a baking sheet.

2. Mix blueberries, 2 tablespoons sugar, cornstarch and basil. Spoon blueberry mixture over pastry to within 2 in. of edge. Fold pastry edge over filling, pleating as you go and leaving the center uncovered.

3. Whisk egg and water; brush over pastry. Sprinkle with remaining sugar. Bake 30 minutes. Sprinkle with goat cheese; bake until the crust is golden and filling bubbly, about 10 minutes. Transfer to a wire rack to cool. Top with torn basil leaves before serving.

PASTRY FOR SINGLE-CRUST PIE (9 INCHES) *Combine 1¼ cups of all-purpose flour and ¼ teaspoon salt; cut in ½ cup cold butter until crumbly. Gradually add 3-5 tablespoons ice water, tossing with a fork until dough holds together when pressed. Wrap in plastic wrap and refrigerate 1 hour.*

NOT YOUR MAMA'S SEVEN-LAYER BARS

The addition of dulce de leche makes this a decadent new take on traditional seven-layer bars. You can cut this recipe in half and make it in an 8x8-inch pan.

—ANDREA BARLOW HOT SPRINGS, AR

PREP: 10 MIN. • **BAKE:** 30 MIN. + COOLING
MAKES: 2 DOZEN

- 24 cream-filled chocolate sandwich cookies
- ½ cup butter, melted
- 1 cup flaked coconut
- 1½ cups crisp brown rice cereal
- 1 can (13.40 ounces) dulce de leche
- 6 tablespoons warm water (110° to 115°)
- 1½ cups coarsely chopped pecans
- ¼ teaspoon sea salt

1. Preheat oven to 350°. Pulse the cookies in food processor until finely chopped. Combine crumbs and melted butter; press onto bottom of greased, foil-lined 13x9-in. baking pan. Spread coconut over crust; sprinkle with crisp rice cereal.

2. Combine dulce de leche and water until smooth. Pour over the cereal. Sprinkle pecans over dulce de leche; press down lightly.

3. Bake until edges are set but the center is still soft, about 30 minutes. (Do not overbake.) Remove from the oven; immediately sprinkle with sea salt. Remove to wire rack to cool completely before cutting into 24 squares.

NOTE *This recipe was tested with Nestle La Lechera dulce de leche; look for it in the international foods section. If using Eagle Brand dulce de leche (caramel flavored sauce), thicken according to package directions before using.*

NOT YOUR MAMA'S SEVEN-LAYER BARS

PECAN PIE THUMBPRINTS

The buttery dough and nutty filling take time to make, but the end result is so worth it. After trying one of these, I think you'll agree.

—PEGGY KEY GRANT, AL

PREP: 30 MIN. + CHILLING
BAKE: 10 MIN./BATCH + COOLING
MAKES: 4½ DOZEN

- 1 cup butter, softened
- ½ cup sugar
- 2 large eggs, separated
- ½ cup dark corn syrup
- 2½ cups all-purpose flour

FILLING
- ¼ cup plus 2 tablespoons confectioners' sugar
- 3 tablespoons butter
- 2 tablespoons dark corn syrup
- ¼ cup plus 2 tablespoons finely chopped pecans

1. In a large bowl, cream butter and sugar until light and fluffy. Beat in egg yolks and corn syrup. Gradually beat in flour. Refrigerate, covered, until firm enough to roll, 30 minutes.

2. For filling, in a small saucepan, combine confectioners' sugar, butter and corn syrup. Bring to a boil over medium heat, stirring occasionally. Remove from heat; stir in pecans. Remove from pan; refrigerate until cold, 30 minutes.

3. Preheat oven to 375°. Shape dough into 1-in. balls; place 2 in. apart on parchment paper-lined baking sheets. In a small bowl, whisk egg whites; brush over tops.

4. Bake 5 minutes. Remove from oven. Gently press an indentation in center of each cookie with the end of a wooden spoon handle. Fill each with a scant ½ teaspoon pecan mixture. Bake until the edges are light brown, 4-5 minutes longer.

5. Cool on pans 5 minutes. Remove to wire racks to cool.

**GRILLED CRANBERRY
PEAR CRUMBLE**
Ronna Farley
Rockville, MD

GRILLED CRANBERRY PEAR CRUMBLE

My husband loves dessert. Fruit crisps are easy, so I make them often! I created this fall-flavored grilled version with fresh pears and items I had on hand.

—**RONNA FARLEY** ROCKVILLE, MD

START TO FINISH: 30 MIN.
MAKES: 6 SERVINGS

- 3 medium ripe pears, sliced
- ½ cup dried cranberries
- ¼ cup sugar
- 2 tablespoons all-purpose flour
- ¼ teaspoon ground cinnamon
- 1 tablespoon butter

TOPPING

- 2 tablespoons butter, melted
- ¼ teaspoon ground cinnamon
- 1 cup granola without raisins

1. Toss the pears and cranberries with sugar, flour and cinnamon. Place 1 tablespoon butter in a 9-in. cast-iron skillet. Place on grill rack over medium heat until butter is melted. Stir in fruit; grill, covered, until pears are tender, 15-20 minutes, stirring occasionally.

2. For topping, mix melted butter and cinnamon; toss with granola. Sprinkle over pears. Grill, covered, 5 minutes. Serve warm.

COCONUT ITALIAN CREAM CAKE

I'd never tasted an Italian cream cake before moving to Colorado. Now I bake for people in the area, and this beauty is one of my most requested treats.

—**ANN BUSH** COLORADO CITY, CO

PREP: 50 MIN. • **BAKE:** 20 MIN. + COOLING
MAKES: 16 SERVINGS

- 5 large eggs, separated
- 1 cup butter, softened
- 1⅔ cups sugar
- 1½ teaspoons vanilla extract
- 2 cups all-purpose flour
- ¾ teaspoon baking soda
- ½ teaspoon salt
- 1 cup buttermilk
- 1⅓ cups flaked coconut
- 1 cup chopped pecans, toasted

COCONUT ITALIAN CREAM CAKE

FROSTING

- 12 ounces cream cheese, softened
- 6 tablespoons butter, softened
- 2¼ teaspoons vanilla extract
- 5⅔ cups confectioners' sugar
- 3 to 4 tablespoons heavy whipping cream
- ½ cup chopped pecans, toasted
- ¼ cup toasted flaked coconut, optional

1. Place the egg whites in a small bowl; let stand at room temperature 30 minutes.

2. Preheat oven to 350°. Line the bottoms of three greased 9-in. round baking pans with parchment paper; grease paper.

3. In a large bowl, cream butter and sugar until light and fluffy. Add egg yolks, one at a time, beating well after each addition. Beat in vanilla. In another bowl, whisk flour, baking soda and salt; add to creamed mixture alternately with buttermilk, beating well after each addition. Fold in coconut and pecans.

4. With clean beaters, beat egg whites on medium speed until stiff peaks form. Gradually fold into batter. Transfer to prepared pans. Bake until a toothpick inserted in center comes out clean, 20-25 minutes. Cool in pans 10 minutes before removing to wire racks; remove paper. Cool completely.

5. For frosting, in a large bowl, beat cream cheese and butter until smooth. Beat in vanilla. Gradually beat in confectioners' sugar and enough cream to reach spreading consistency. Spread frosting between layers and over top and sides of cake. Sprinkle with pecans and, if desired, coconut. Refrigerate leftovers.

NOTE *To toast pecans and coconut, spread each, one at a time, in a 15x10x1-in. baking pan. Bake at 350°, stirring occasionally, until lightly browned, 5-10 minutes.*

NANA'S CHOCOLATE CUPCAKES WITH MINT FROSTING

These cupcakes remind me of when Nana used to make them at Christmas every year. Even though she is no longer with us, it brings me joy baking them because it gives the cakes special meaning. For a more indulgent version, double the frosting and pile it high on top of each cupcake.

—**CHEKOTA HUNTER** CASSVILLE, MO

PREP: 25 MIN. • **BAKE:** 15 MIN. + COOLING
MAKES: 1 DOZEN

- ½ cup baking cocoa
- 1 cup boiling water
- ¼ cup butter, softened
- 1 cup sugar
- 2 large eggs
- 1⅓ cups all-purpose flour
- 2 teaspoons baking powder
- ¼ teaspoon salt
- ¼ cup unsweetened applesauce

FROSTING

- 1 cup confectioners' sugar
- 3 tablespoons butter, softened
- 4 teaspoons heavy whipping cream
  Dash peppermint extract
- 1 drop green food coloring, optional
- 2 tablespoons miniature semisweet chocolate chips
  Mint Andes candies, optional

1. Preheat oven to 375°. Line 12 muffin cups with paper or foil liners. Mix cocoa and boiling water until smooth; cool completely.

2. Beat butter and sugar together until blended. Beat in eggs, one at a time. In another bowl, whisk together flour, baking powder and salt; add to butter mixture alternately with applesauce, beating well after each addition. Beat in cocoa mixture.

3. Fill the prepared muffin cups three-fourths full. Bake until a toothpick inserted in center comes out clean, 15-18 minutes. Cool for 10 minutes before removing to a wire rack to cool completely.

4. Beat confectioners' sugar, butter, cream and extract until smooth. If desired, tint frosting green with food coloring. Stir in chocolate chips. Spread over cupcakes. If desired, top with candies.

**BACON CHOCOLATE CHIP
CHEESECAKE BLONDIES**

BACON CHOCOLATE CHIP CHEESECAKE BLONDIES

If you're a sweet and savory fan like myself, you'll absolutely love these. There's not much better than a cookie, brownie and cheesecake all mixed up together with bacon to top it off.
—**KATIE O'KEEFFE** DERRY, NH

PREP: 30 MIN. • **BAKE:** 45 MIN. + CHILLING
MAKES: 16 SERVINGS

- 8 **bacon strips, cooked and crumbled**
- 1 **cup butter, softened**
- ¾ **cup sugar**
- ¾ **cup packed brown sugar**
- 2 **large eggs**
- 1 **teaspoon vanilla extract**
- 2¼ **cups all-purpose flour**
- 1 **teaspoon salt**
- 1 **teaspoon baking soda**
- 2 **cups (12 ounces) semisweet chocolate chips**

CHEESECAKE LAYER
- 2 **packages (8 ounces each) cream cheese, softened**
- 1 **cup sugar**
- 2 **large eggs**
- ¾ **cup 2% milk**
- 2 **teaspoons vanilla extract**

1. Preheat oven to 375°. Line a 9-in. square baking pan with foil, letting ends extend up sides; grease foil.
2. Reserve ¼ cup crumbled bacon for top. In a large bowl, cream butter and sugars until light and fluffy. Beat in eggs and vanilla. In another bowl, whisk flour, salt and baking soda; gradually beat into creamed mixture. Stir in chocolate chips and remaining bacon. Press half of the dough onto bottom of prepared pan.
3. For cheesecake layer, in a large bowl, beat cream cheese and sugar until smooth. Add eggs, milk and vanilla; beat on low speed just until blended. Pour over dough in prepared pan; drop the remaining dough by rounded tablespoons over cheesecake layer. Sprinkle with reserved bacon.
4. Bake 45-50 minutes or until golden brown. Cool in pan on a wire rack. Refrigerate at least 4 hours before cutting. Lifting with foil, remove from pan. Cut into bars.

CARROT CAKE WITH PECAN FROSTING

This impressive cake is one of my husband's favorites. It's homey and old-fashioned—perfect for special holidays or Sunday family dinners.
—**ADRIAN BADON** DENHAM SPRINGS, LA

PREP: 35 MIN. • **BAKE:** 40 MIN. + COOLING
MAKES: 16 SERVINGS

- 1 **cup shortening**
- 2 **cups sugar**
- 4 **large eggs**
- 1 **can (8 ounces) unsweetened crushed pineapple, undrained**
- 2½ **cups all-purpose flour**
- 2 **teaspoons ground cinnamon**
- 1 **teaspoon baking powder**
- 1 **teaspoon baking soda**
- ¾ **teaspoon salt**
- 3 **cups shredded carrots (about 6 medium carrots)**

FROSTING
- 1 **package (8 ounces) reduced-fat cream cheese**
- ½ **cup butter, softened**
- 1 **teaspoon vanilla extract**
- 3¾ **cups confectioners' sugar**
- 1 **cup chopped pecans**

1. Preheat oven to 325°. Line bottoms of two greased 9-in. round baking pans with parchment paper; grease the paper.
2. In a large bowl, cream shortening and sugar until fluffy. Add the eggs, one at a time, beating well after each addition. Beat in pineapple. In another bowl, whisk flour, cinnamon, baking powder, baking soda and salt; gradually add to creamed mixture. Stir in carrots.
3. Transfer batter to prepared pans. Bake until a toothpick inserted in center comes out clean, 40-45 minutes. Cool in pans 10 minutes before removing to wire racks; remove paper. Cool completely.
4. In a large bowl, beat cream cheese, butter and vanilla until blended. Gradually beat in confectioners' sugar until smooth. Stir in pecans.
5. Spread frosting between layers and over top and sides of cake. Refrigerate until serving.

BERRIES & CREAM TRIFLES

Layers of cubed cake, berries and creamy ricotta mixture make pretty trifles that taste as rich as cheesecake.
—**JOAN DUCKWORTH** LEE'S SUMMIT, MO

PREP: 30 MIN. • **COOK:** 10 MIN. + CHILLING
MAKES: 8 SERVINGS

- 2 **cups fresh or frozen cranberries**
- 1 **cup fresh or frozen blueberries**
- ½ **cup sugar**
- ½ **cup water**
- 1 **cup whole-milk ricotta cheese**
- 4 **ounces cream cheese, cubed and softened**
- ¼ **cup confectioners' sugar**
- ½ **teaspoon vanilla extract**
- 1 **loaf (10¾ ounces) frozen pound cake, thawed and cut into ½-inch cubes**

1. In a small saucepan, combine cranberries, blueberries, sugar and water; bring to a boil, stirring to dissolve sugar. Reduce heat; simmer, uncovered, 5 minutes. Transfer to a small bowl; cool completely. Refrigerate, covered, at least 1 hour or until cold.

2. Place the ricotta cheese, cream cheese, confectioners' sugar and vanilla in a small food processor. Process until smooth.

3. In each of eight parfait glasses, layer 1 tablespoon berry sauce, ⅓ cup cake cubes, 2 tablespoons ricotta mixture and 2 tablespoons berry sauce. Repeat cake and cheese layers; top with 1 tablespoon berry sauce. Refrigerate, covered, until serving or up to 2 hours.

GOES GREAT WITH

Dig into Creamy Chicken & Broccoli Stew, page 71, before enjoying these treats as a refreshing finale.

CHUNKY APPLE-CINNAMON CAKE

Here's a nice change of pace from apple pie that's tasty and worthy of a special get-together. It's very easy to make. Add a scoop of ice cream if you like.
—**ELLEN RUZINSKY** YORKTOWN HEIGHTS, NY

PREP: 25 MIN. • **BAKE:** 45 MIN. + COOLING
MAKES: 15 SERVINGS

- 2¾ **pounds McIntosh, Jonathan or Granny Smith apples, peeled and thinly sliced (11 cups)**
- ½ **cup packed brown sugar**
- 3 **teaspoons ground cinnamon, divided**
- 1 **cup plus 1 tablespoon sugar, divided**
- 1 **cup canola oil**
- 4 **large eggs**
- 3 **tablespoons orange juice**
- 2 **teaspoons vanilla extract**
- 2½ **cups all-purpose flour**
- 2 **teaspoons baking powder**
- ½ **teaspoon kosher salt**

1. Preheat oven to 425°. In a large bowl, toss apples with brown sugar and 2 teaspoons cinnamon.

2. In a large bowl, beat 1 cup sugar, oil, eggs, orange juice and vanilla until well blended. In another bowl, whisk the flour, baking powder and salt; gradually beat into sugar mixture.

3. Transfer half of the batter to an ungreased 13x9-in. baking pan. Top with apples. Spread remaining batter over apples. Mix remaining sugar and cinnamon; sprinkle over top. Bake 10 minutes.

4. Reduce oven setting to 375°. Bake until golden brown and the apples are tender, 35-45 minutes. Cool on a wire rack.

CHUNKY APPLE-CINNAMON CAKE

HUMBLE BUMBLE CRUMBLE BARS

ORANGE DREAM MINI CUPCAKES

The bright taste of these cute cupcakes reminds me and my friends of orange-and-vanilla frozen treats.

—**JEN SHEPHERD** ST. PETERS, MO

PREP: 1 HOUR • **BAKE:** 15 MIN. + COOLING
MAKES: 4 DOZEN

- ½ cup butter, softened
- 1 cup sugar
- 2 large eggs
- 1 tablespoon grated orange peel
- 1 tablespoon orange juice
- ½ teaspoon vanilla extract
- 1½ cups all-purpose flour
- 1½ teaspoons baking powder
- ¼ teaspoon salt
- ½ cup buttermilk

BUTTERCREAM

- ½ cup butter, softened
- ¼ teaspoon salt
- 2 cups confectioners' sugar
- 2 tablespoons 2% milk
- 1½ teaspoons vanilla extract
- ½ cup orange marmalade

1. Preheat oven to 325°. Line 48 mini-muffin cups with paper liners. In a large bowl, cream butter and sugar until light and fluffy. Add eggs, one at a time, beating well after each addition. Beat in orange peel, orange juice and vanilla. In another bowl, whisk flour, baking powder and salt; add to creamed mixture alternately with buttermilk, beating well after each addition.
2. Fill prepared cups two-thirds full. Bake until a toothpick inserted in center comes out clean, 11-13 minutes. Cool in pans 5 minutes; remove to wire racks to cool completely.
3. For buttercream, in a large bowl, beat butter and salt until creamy. Gradually beat in confectioners' sugar, milk and vanilla until smooth.
4. Using a paring knife, cut a 1-in.-wide cone-shaped piece from top of each cupcake; discard removed portion. Fill cavity with marmalade. Pipe or spread buttercream over tops.

HUMBLE BUMBLE CRUMBLE BARS

While developing a treat for my bingo group, I asked my husband for ideas. He suggested a fruity bar. This berry bar is lightly sweet and so easy.

—**NANCY PHILLIPS** PORTLAND, ME

PREP: 30 MIN. • **BAKE:** 45 MIN. + COOLING
MAKES: 15 SERVINGS

- ½ cup butter, softened
- ¾ cup sugar
- 1 large egg
- 2½ cups all-purpose flour
- ½ teaspoon baking powder
- ¼ teaspoon salt
- ¼ cup packed brown sugar
- 1 teaspoon ground cinnamon

FILLING

- 2 cups chunky applesauce
- ½ teaspoon ground cinnamon
- ⅛ teaspoon ground nutmeg
- 2 cups fresh blackberries
- 2 cups fresh raspberries

1. Preheat oven to 350°. In a large bowl, cream butter and sugar until light and fluffy. Beat in egg. In another bowl, whisk flour, baking powder and salt; gradually beat into creamed mixture. Reserve ½ cup crumb mixture for topping. Press remaining mixture onto bottom of a greased 13x9-in. baking pan. Bake until lightly browned, 12-15 minutes. Cool on a wire rack.
2. Stir brown sugar and cinnamon into reserved topping; set aside. In a large bowl, combine applesauce, cinnamon and nutmeg until blended. Spread over crust; top with berries and reserved topping. Bake until golden brown, 30-35 minutes. Cool in pan on a wire rack. Cut into bars.

Sunday Extras

With a little of this and a little of that, this chapter has just what you need to either start or complete a meal. Any of these tasty appetizers and refreshing beverages will bring in the raves!

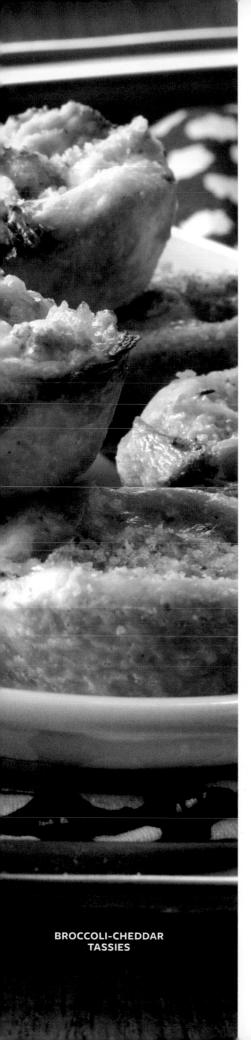

BROCCOLI-CHEDDAR TASSIES

Our family just adores broccoli casserole. I wanted to try it as an appetizer, so I used a pecan tassie recipe for the crust. The result? We're talking scrumptious.
—**GAIL GAISER** EWING, NJ

PREP: 45 MIN. + CHILLING
BAKE: 20 MIN./BATCH
MAKES: ABOUT 4 DOZEN

- 1 **cup butter, softened**
- 6 **ounces cream cheese, softened**
- 2 **cups all-purpose flour**

FILLING

- 1 **package (16 ounces) frozen chopped broccoli**
- 1 **large egg, lightly beaten**
- 1 **can (10¾ ounces) condensed cream of celery soup, undiluted**
- ¼ **cup 2% milk**
- ¼ **cup mayonnaise**
- ½ **cup shredded sharp cheddar cheese**

TOPPING

- ¼ **cup dry bread crumbs**
- 1 **tablespoon butter, melted**

1. In a small bowl, cream butter and cream cheese until smooth. Gradually beat flour into creamed mixture. Divide the dough in half. Shape each into a disk; wrap in plastic wrap. Refrigerate 1 hour or until firm enough to handle.
2. Preheat oven to 350°. Shape dough into 1-in. balls; place in greased mini-muffin cups. Using floured fingers, press evenly onto bottoms and up sides of cups.
3. Cook the broccoli according to package directions; drain. In a large bowl, combine the egg, condensed soup, milk and mayonnaise; stir in cheese and cooked broccoli. Spoon about 1 tablespoon filling into each cup. For the topping, mix bread crumbs and melted butter; sprinkle over filling.
4. Bake until the edges are golden brown, 18-22 minutes. Cool in pans 2 minutes before removing to wire racks. Serve warm.

TO MAKE AHEAD *Dough can be made 2 days in advance.*
FREEZE OPTION *Freeze cooled pastries on waxed paper-lined baking sheets until firm. Transfer to resealable plastic freezer bags. To use, reheat pastries on ungreased baking sheets in a preheated 350° oven until lightly browned and heated through, 14-16 minutes.*

⑤ INGREDIENTS FAST FIX ▸

FRESH-SQUEEZED PINK LEMONADE

There's a balance of sweet and tart in this refreshing beverage. It becomes perfectly pink with the addition of grape juice.
—**CINDY BARTNICKI** MOUNT PROSPECT, IL

START TO FINISH: 15 MIN.
MAKES: 6 SERVINGS

- 4 **cups water, divided**
- 1 **cup sugar**
- 3 **lemon peel strips**
- 1 **cup lemon juice (about 5 lemons)**
- 1 **tablespoon grape juice**
  Lemon slices and maraschino cherries, optional

1. In a small saucepan, bring 2 cups water, sugar and lemon peel to a boil. Reduce the heat; cover and simmer for 5 minutes. Remove from the heat. Discard lemon peel.
2. In a large pitcher, combine the remaining water, lemon juice, grape juice and sugar mixture. Serve over ice. Garnish with lemon slices and cherries if desired.
FRESH-SQUEEZED LEMONADE *Omit grape juice.*

GOES GREAT WITH
Keep dinner light and sweet when you pair lemonade with Southern Corn Bread Salad, page 53.

BROCCOLI-CHEDDAR TASSIES

SWEET & SPICY JALAPENO POPPERS

FAST FIX

SWEET & SPICY JALAPENO POPPERS

There's no faster way to get a party started than with these bacon-wrapped poppers. Make them ahead and bake just before serving.

—DAWN ONUFFER CRESTVIEW, FL

START TO FINISH: 30 MIN.
MAKES: 1 DOZEN

- 6 jalapeno peppers
- 4 ounces cream cheese, softened
- 2 tablespoons shredded cheddar cheese
- 6 bacon strips, halved widthwise
- ¼ cup packed brown sugar
- 1 tablespoon chili seasoning mix

1. Cut jalapenos in half lengthwise and remove seeds; set aside. In a small bowl, beat cheeses until blended. Spoon into pepper halves. Wrap a half-strip of bacon around each pepper half.
2. Combine brown sugar and chili seasoning; coat peppers with sugar mixture. Place in a greased 15x10x1-in. baking pan.
3. Bake at 350° until bacon is firm, 18-20 minutes.
NOTE *Wear disposable gloves when cutting hot peppers; the oils can burn skin. Avoid touching your face.*

⑤ INGREDIENTS | FAST FIX

WARM & COZY SPICED CIDER

We take winter seriously in Minnesota. This comforting cider flavored with cinnamon, cloves and fruit juices helps warm and brace our spirits.

—CHRIS RUNYAN MONTEVIDEO, MN

START TO FINISH: 30 MIN.
MAKES: 10 SERVINGS (¾ CUP EACH)

- 2 quarts unsweetened apple cider
- 1 cup orange juice
- 1 can (5½ ounces) apricot nectar
- 1 teaspoon ground cinnamon
- ⅛ teaspoon ground cloves

In a 6-qt. stockpot, combine all ingredients. Bring to a boil. Reduce heat; simmer, uncovered, 15 minutes to allow flavors to blend. Serve warm.

SLOW COOKER
SPINACH &
ARTICHOKE
DIP

SMOKED SALMON DEVILED EGGS

Flaky salmon and creamy sauce go so well over hard-boiled eggs. Drizzle the sauce or serve it on the side—it's fantastic either way.

—**MARINELA DRAGAN** PORTLAND, OR

PREP: 30 MIN. • **COOK:** 20 MIN.
MAKES: 32 APPETIZERS

16 **hard-cooked large eggs**
 4 **ounces cream cheese, softened**
 ⅓ **cup mayonnaise**
 2 **tablespoons snipped fresh dill**
 1 **tablespoon capers, drained and finely chopped**
 1 **tablespoon lemon juice**
 1 **teaspoon horseradish sauce**
 1 **teaspoon prepared mustard**
 ½ **teaspoon freshly ground pepper**
 ¾ **cup flaked smoked salmon fillet**
SAUCE
 1 **cup mayonnaise**
 ¼ **cup plus 2 tablespoons ketchup**
 1 **tablespoon horseradish sauce**
 1 **tablespoon prepared mustard**
 ¼ **cup smoked salmon fillets, optional**

1. Cut the eggs lengthwise in half. Remove yolks, reserving whites. In a small bowl, mash yolks. Mix in cream cheese, mayonnaise, dill, capers, lemon juice, horseradish sauce, mustard and pepper. Fold in salmon. Spoon into egg whites. Refrigerate, covered, until serving.
2. For sauce, mix the mayonnaise, ketchup, horseradish sauce and mustard. If desired, top eggs with salmon mixture; serve with sauce.

✳

TEST KITCHEN TIP
You can keep unpeeled hard-cooked eggs in the refrigerator for one week. Once peeled, use eggs immediately.

SLOW COOKER
SLOW COOKER SPINACH & ARTICHOKE DIP

With this creamy dip, I can get my daughters to eat spinach and artichokes. We serve it with chips, toasted pita bread or fresh veggies.

—**JENNIFER STOWELL** MONTEZUMA, IA

PREP: 10 MIN. • **COOK:** 2 HOURS
MAKES: 32 SERVINGS (¼ CUP EACH)

 2 **cans (14 ounces each) water-packed artichoke hearts, drained and chopped**
 2 **packages (10 ounces each) frozen chopped spinach, thawed and squeezed dry**
 1 **jar (15 ounces) Alfredo sauce**
 1 **package (8 ounces) cream cheese, cubed**
 2 **cups shredded Italian cheese blend**
 1 **cup shredded part-skim mozzarella cheese**
 1 **cup shredded Parmesan cheese**
 1 **cup 2% milk**
 2 **garlic cloves, minced**
   Assorted crackers and/or cucumber slices

In a greased 4-qt. slow cooker, combine the first nine ingredients. Cook, covered, on low 2-3 hours or until heated through. Serve with crackers and/or cucumber slices.

FAST FIX
FRUIT KABOBS WITH CREAM CHEESE DIP

These fruity kabobs are so refreshing. They're quick and easy to make, too.
—**KATHLEEN HEDGER** GODFREY, IL

START TO FINISH: 15 MIN.
MAKES: 6 KABOBS (1¼ CUPS DIP)

 6 **ounces cream cheese, softened**
 ⅓ **cup confectioners' sugar**
 ⅓ **cup sour cream**
 ¼ **teaspoon almond extract**
12 **fresh strawberries, trimmed**
12 **green grapes**
12 **fresh pineapple cubes (1 inch)**

In a small bowl, beat cream cheese, confectioners' sugar, sour cream and extract until smooth. Refrigerate until serving. On six wooden skewers, alternately thread strawberries, grapes and pineapple. Serve with dip.

BAKED BABY POTATOES WITH OLIVE PESTO

Pack all the appeal of a baked potato into the perfect bite-sized appetizer. I top off each one with a dollop of sour cream and coarsely ground pepper.

—SARAH SHAIKH MUMBAI, INDIA

PREP: 35 MIN. • BAKE: 30 MIN.
MAKES: ABOUT 3 DOZEN

- 3 pounds baby red potatoes (1¾ inches wide, about 36)
- 6 tablespoons olive oil, divided
- 2 teaspoons salt
- 1½ cups pimiento-stuffed olives
- ½ cup chopped onion
- ¼ cup pine nuts, toasted
- 2 garlic cloves, minced
- ½ cup sour cream
  Coarsely ground pepper, optional

1. Preheat oven to 400°. Place potatoes in a large bowl. Add 2 tablespoons oil and salt; toss to coat. Transfer to a greased 15x10x1-in. baking pan. Bake until tender, 30-35 minutes.
2. Meanwhile, place olives, onion, pine nuts and garlic in a food processor; pulse until chopped. Gradually add remaining oil; process to reach desired consistency.
3. When potatoes are cool enough to handle, cut thin slices off bottoms to allow potatoes to sit upright. Cut an "X" in the top of each potato; squeeze sides to open tops slightly. Place on a serving platter.
4. Spoon olive pesto onto potatoes; top with sour cream. If desired, sprinkle with pepper. Serve warm.

NOTE *To toast nuts, bake in a shallow pan in a 350° oven for 5-10 minutes or cook in a skillet over low heat, stirring occasionally, until lightly browned.*

MARYLAND CORN POPS

MARYLAND CORN POPS

Fresh-picked sweet corn is a big thing in Maryland. Here's my homespun version of Mexican street corn that brings in local Bay flavors.

—KRISTIE SCHLEY SEVERNA PARK, MD

PREP: 25 MIN. • GRILL: 10 MIN.
MAKES: 2 DOZEN

- 8 medium ears sweet corn, husks removed
- 2 tablespoons canola oil
- 1½ cups mayonnaise
- 1½ teaspoons garlic powder
- ¼ teaspoon freshly ground pepper
- 24 corncob holders
- 2 cups crumbled feta cheese
- 2 tablespoons seafood seasoning
- ¼ cup minced fresh cilantro
  Lime wedges, optional

1. Brush all sides of corn with oil. Grill, covered, over medium heat, turning occasionally, until tender and lightly browned, 10-12 minutes. Remove from grill; cool slightly.
2. Meanwhile, in a small bowl, mix mayonnaise, garlic powder and pepper. Cut each ear of corn into thirds. Insert one corncob holder into each piece. Spread corn with the mayonnaise mixture; sprinkle with cheese, seafood seasoning and cilantro. If desired, serve with lime wedges.

SLOW COOKER CHEDDAR BACON BEER DIP

My tangy, smoky dip won top prize at our office party recipe contest. Other beers can work, but steer clear of dark varieties.
—**ASHLEY LECKER** GREEN BAY, WI

PREP: 15 MIN. • **COOK:** 3 HOURS
MAKES: 4½ CUPS

- 18 **ounces cream cheese, softened**
- ¼ **cup sour cream**
- 1½ **tablespoons Dijon mustard**
- 1 **teaspoon garlic powder**
- 1 **cup amber beer or nonalcoholic beer**
- 2 **cups shredded cheddar cheese**
- 1 **pound cooked and crumbled bacon strips, divided**
- ¼ **cup heavy whipping cream**
- 1 **green onion, thinly sliced**
  Soft pretzel bites

1. In a greased 3-qt. slow cooker, combine cream cheese, sour cream, mustard and garlic powder until smooth. Stir in beer, cheese and all but 2 tablespoons bacon. Cook, covered, on low, stirring occasionally, until heated through, 3-4 hours.

2. In the last 30 minutes, stir in heavy cream. Top with onion and remaining bacon. Serve with pretzel bun bites.

★ ★ ★ ★ ★ **READER REVIEW**

"Oh my goodness, this recipe was a hit. I baked freezer pretzels, cut into bite-sized pieces, instead of the pretzel buns. Will definitely make again!"

EJSHELLABARGER TASTEOFHOME.COM

SLOW COOKER CHEDDAR BACON BEER DIP

BREADSTICK
PIZZA

BREADSTICK PIZZA

Dig into a hassle-free homemade pizza featuring refrigerated breadsticks as the crust. Feeding kids? Slice pieces into small strips and let them dip each strip into marinara sauce. They'll love it!

—**MARY HANKINS** KANSAS CITY, MO

PREP: 25 MIN. • **BAKE:** 20 MIN.
MAKES: 12 SERVINGS

- 2 **tubes (11 ounces each) refrigerated breadsticks**
- ½ **pound sliced fresh mushrooms**
- 2 **medium green peppers, chopped**
- 1 **medium onion, chopped**
- 1½ **teaspoons Italian seasoning, divided**
- 4 **teaspoons olive oil, divided**
- 1½ **cups shredded cheddar cheese, divided**
- 5 **ounces Canadian bacon, chopped**
- 1½ **cups shredded part-skim mozzarella cheese**
   Marinara sauce

1. Unroll breadsticks into a greased 15x10x1-in. baking pan. Press onto the bottom and up the sides of pan; pinch seams to seal. Bake at 350° until set, 6-8 minutes.
2. Meanwhile, in a large skillet, saute the mushrooms, peppers, onion and 1 teaspoon of the Italian seasoning in 2 teaspoons oil until vegetables are crisp-tender; drain.
3. Brush crust with remaining oil. Sprinkle with ¾ cup cheddar cheese; top with vegetable mixture and Canadian bacon. Combine mozzarella cheese and remaining cheddar cheese; sprinkle over top. Sprinkle with remaining Italian seasoning.
4. Bake until cheese is melted and crust is golden brown, 20-25 minutes. Serve with marinara sauce.
FREEZE OPTION *Bake crust as directed, add toppings and cool. Securely wrap and freeze unbaked pizza. To use, unwrap pizza; bake as directed, increasing time as necessary.*

PASTRAMI ROLL-UPS
Merritt Heinrich
Oswego, IL

---

⑤ INGREDIENTS **FAST FIX**
PASTRAMI ROLL-UPS

For a book club event, I created pastrami roll-ups with cream cheese and a pickle. Those tasty roll-ups quickly pulled a disappearing act.

—**MERRITT HEINRICH** OSWEGO, IL

START TO FINISH: 15 MIN.
MAKES: 4 DOZEN

- ¾ **cup spreadable cream cheese**
- ½ **cup crumbled blue cheese**
- 12 **slices lean deli pastrami**
- 12 **dill pickle spears**

1. In a small bowl, mix cream cheese and blue cheese until blended. If necessary, pat pastrami and pickles dry with paper towels.
2. Spread about 1 tablespoon cheese mixture over each pastrami slice; top with a pickle spear. Roll up tightly. Cut each roll into four slices. Refrigerate leftovers.

---

⑤ INGREDIENTS **FAST FIX**
REFRESHING RASPBERRY ICED TEA

Because this iced tea recipe makes a gallon, it's a nice choice for parties. Make it ahead and freeze it so you can serve it later.

—**ARLANA HENDRICKS** MANCHESTER, TN

START TO FINISH: 20 MIN.
MAKES: 16 SERVINGS (1 CUP EACH)

- 6 **cups water**
- 1¾ **cups sugar**
- 8 **individual tea bags**
- ¾ **cup frozen apple-raspberry juice concentrate**
- 8 **cups cold water**
   Ice cubes
   Fresh raspberries, optional

In a large saucepan, bring 6 cups water and sugar to a boil; remove from the heat. Add tea bags; steep, covered, 3-5 minutes according to taste. Discard tea bags. Add juice concentrate; stir in cold water. Serve over ice, with raspberries if desired.

CRAB CAKES WITH PEANUT SAUCE

Crab cakes are a go-to on my party food list. The peanut sauce in this recipe takes the cake!

—AMBER MASSEY ARGYLE, TX

PREP: 25 MIN. + CHILLING
COOK: 5 MIN./BATCH
MAKES: 1 DOZEN (⅓ CUP SAUCE)

- ¼ cup rice vinegar
- 2 tablespoons creamy peanut butter
- 1 garlic clove, minced
- 1 teaspoon brown sugar
- 1 teaspoon olive oil
- ¼ teaspoon ground mustard
  Dash cayenne pepper

CRAB CAKES
- 1 cup plain Greek yogurt
- ⅔ cup crushed saltines (about 15 crackers)
- ¼ cup finely chopped celery
- ¼ cup finely chopped roasted sweet red pepper
- ¼ cup minced fresh parsley
- 2 tablespoons finely chopped onion
- 1 large egg white, lightly beaten
- 1 tablespoon fresh lemon juice
- 2 teaspoons prepared horseradish
- ½ teaspoon paprika
- ¼ teaspoon salt
- 1 pound lump crabmeat, drained
- 1 tablespoon olive oil
  Minced fresh chives

1. In a small bowl, whisk the first seven ingredients until blended. Set aside.
2. In a large bowl, mix the first 11 crab cake ingredients until blended. Fold in crab. Shape mixture into twelve ½-in.-thick patties. Refrigerate, covered, 30 minutes.
3. In a large skillet, heat 1 tablespoon oil over medium-high heat. Add crab cakes in batches; cook 2-3 minutes on each side or until golden brown. Sprinkle with chives; serve with sauce.

GOES GREAT WITH

To turn these crab cakes into the main dish, simply serve them alongside a salad or side dish. And turn to page 82 to pick out the perfect dessert!

FRIED PROSCIUTTO TORTELLINI

My take on Italian street food, these fried tortellini are crunchy, ooey-gooey good. For the sauce, use the best quality tomatoes you can find.

—ANGELA LEMOINE HOWELL, NJ

PREP: 25 MIN. • **COOK:** 5 MIN./BATCH
MAKES: ABOUT 3½ DOZEN

- 2 large eggs
- 2 tablespoons 2% milk
- ⅔ cup seasoned bread crumbs
- 1 teaspoon garlic powder
- 2 tablespoons grated Pecorino Romano cheese
- 1 tablespoon minced fresh parsley
- ½ teaspoon salt
  Oil for frying
- 1 package (12 ounces) refrigerated prosciutto ricotta tortellini

TOMATO SAUCE
- 1 tablespoon olive oil
- 3 tablespoons finely chopped onion
- 4 garlic cloves, coarsely chopped
- 1 can (15 ounces) tomato puree
- 1 tablespoon minced fresh basil
- ¼ teaspoon salt
- ¼ teaspoon pepper
  Additional minced fresh basil

1. Whisk together eggs and milk. In another bowl, stir together the next five ingredients.
2. In an electric skillet, heat ¼-in. oil to 375°. Dip tortellini in egg mixture, then in the bread crumb mixture to coat. Fry tortellini in batches, adding oil as necessary, until golden brown, 1½ to 2 minutes each side. Drain on paper towels.
3. Meanwhile, in a small saucepan, heat 1 tablespoon olive oil over medium heat. Add onion and garlic, cooking until softened. Stir in tomato puree, basil, salt and pepper; bring to a boil. Reduce heat; simmer, uncovered, 10 minutes. Sprinkle with minced fresh basil.
4. Serve tortellini with tomato sauce for dipping.

FRIED PROSCIUTTO TORTELLINI

WHITE PIZZA DIP

I first served this dip during a football party, and boy, did it disappear fast. It's a great addition to a snack table because it can be made ahead of time and refrigerated until you're ready to pop it in the oven.

—**MOLLY SEIDEL** EDGEWOOD, NM

PREP: 10 MIN. • **BAKE:** 35 MIN.
MAKES: 12 SERVINGS (¼ CUP EACH)

- 2 cups (16 ounces) sour cream
- 1 cup whole-milk ricotta cheese
- 1 cup (4 ounces) shredded part-skim mozzarella cheese, divided
- ¼ cup chopped pepperoni
- 1 envelope Lipton savory herb with garlic soup mix
  French bread baguette slices, toasted

1. Preheat oven to 350°. In a small bowl, mix sour cream, ricotta cheese, ¾ cup mozzarella cheese, pepperoni and soup mix until blended. Spread into a greased 9-in. pie plate. Sprinkle with remaining mozzarella cheese.
2. Bake, uncovered, 35-40 minutes or until bubbly. Serve with the baguette slices.

BACON CHEESEBURGER SLIDER BAKE

I created this dish to fill two pans because these sliders disappear in a flash. Just cut the recipe in half if you only need one pan's worth.

—**NICK IVERSON** MILWAUKEE, WI

PREP: 20 MIN. • **BAKE:** 25 MIN.
MAKES: 2 DOZEN

- 2 packages (18 ounces each) Hawaiian sweet rolls
- 4 cups shredded cheddar cheese, divided
- 2 pounds ground beef
- 1 cup chopped onion
- 1 can (14½ ounces) diced tomatoes with garlic and onion, drained
- 1 tablespoon Dijon mustard
- 1 tablespoon Worcestershire sauce
- ¾ teaspoon salt
- ¾ teaspoon pepper
- 24 bacon strips, cooked and crumbled

GLAZE
- 1 cup butter, cubed
- ¼ cup packed brown sugar
- 4 teaspoons Worcestershire sauce
- 2 tablespoons Dijon mustard
- 2 tablespoons sesame seeds

1. Preheat oven to 350°. Without separating rolls, cut each package of rolls horizontally in half; arrange the bottom halves in two greased 13x9-in. baking pans. Sprinkle each pan of rolls with 1 cup cheese. Bake 3-5 minutes or until cheese is melted.
2. In a large skillet, cook beef and onion over medium heat 6-8 minutes or until beef is no longer pink and onion is tender, breaking up beef into crumbles; drain. Stir in tomatoes, mustard, Worcestershire sauce, salt and pepper. Cook and stir 1-2 minutes or until combined.
3. Spoon beef mixture evenly over rolls; sprinkle with remaining cheese. Top with bacon. Replace tops. For glaze, in a microwave-safe bowl combine the butter, brown sugar, Worcestershire sauce and mustard.

Microwave, covered, on high until butter is melted, stirring occasionally. Pour over rolls; sprinkle with sesame seeds. Bake, uncovered, 20-25 minutes or until golden brown and heated through.

FREEZE OPTION *Cover and freeze unbaked sandwiches; prepare and freeze glaze. To use, partially thaw in refrigerator overnight. Remove from the refrigerator 30 minutes before baking. Preheat oven to 350°. Pour glaze over buns and sprinkle with sesame seeds. Bake the sandwiches as directed, increasing time by 10-15 minutes or until the cheese is melted and a thermometer inserted in the center reads 165°.*

TEST KITCHEN TIP
You can lighten up these sliders easily by using ground turkey in place of ground beef and halve the glaze. The end result is just as delicious!

BACON CHEESEBURGER SLIDER BAKE
Nick Iverson
Milwaukee, WI

General Index

MAPLE
Maple-Sage Brined Turkey, 13
Maple-Walnut Sweet Potatoes, 56
Roasted Apple Salad with Spicy Maple-Cider
   Vinaigrette, 52

MEAT LOAF & MEAT PIES
Beef Potato Meat Loaf, 9
Butternut Squash, Cauliflower & Beef
   Shepherd's Pie, 11
Chicken Biscuit Potpie, 22
My Mom's Best Meat Loaf, 10
Puff Pastry Chicken Potpie, 35

MEATLESS MAIN DISHES
Artichoke Florentine Pasta, 18
Eggplant & Zucchini Rollatini, 38

NUTS & PEANUT BUTTER
Almond Turkey Casserole, 30
Coconut Italian Cream Cake, 93
Crab Cakes with Peanut Sauce, 106
Cranberry Pecan Oatmeal Cookies, 83
Easy Four-Layer Chocolate Dessert, 88
Maple-Walnut Sweet Potatoes, 56
Not Your Mama's Seven-Layer Bars, 91
Pecan Pie Thumbprints, 91
Roasted Green Beans with Lemon & Walnuts, 62

OATS
Cranberry Pecan Oatmeal Cookies, 83

OLIVES
Baked Baby Potatoes with Olive Pesto, 102
Olive & Onion Quick Bread, 78

ONIONS
Olive & Onion Quick Bread, 78
Orange-Glazed Carrots, Onions & Radishes, 66
Zucchini Onion Pie, 67

ORANGE
Orange Dream Mini Cupcakes, 97
Orange-Glazed Carrots, Onions & Radishes, 66
Orange-Glazed Pork with Sweet Potatoes, 18
Orange Spice Carrots, 57
Ribbon Salad with Orange Vinaigrette, 50

OVEN ENTREES
Alfredo-Pancetta Stuffed Shells, 12
Almond Turkey Casserole, 30
Baked Orange Roughy & Rice, 33
Baked Simple Meatball Stroganoff, 37
Balsamic Roast Chicken, 7
Beef Potato Meat Loaf, 9
Butternut Squash, Cauliflower & Beef Shepherd's
   Pie, 11
Chicken Biscuit Potpie, 22
Chicken Cordon Bleu Bake, 28
Chicken Tamale Bake, 36
Chili Beef Corn Bread Casserole, 27
Citrus-Molasses Glazed Ham, 20
Easy Cheesy Loaded Grits, 25
Eggplant & Zucchini Rollatini, 38
Fourth of July Bean Casserole, 32

Ham & Veggie Casserole, 27
Hearty Beef Casserole, 33
Herb-Roasted Salmon Fillets, 10
Hot Chicken Casserole, 25
Maple-Sage Brined Turkey, 13
Mini Reuben Casseroles, 30
My Mom's Best Meat Loaf, 10
New England Bean & Bog Cassoulet, 29
Orange-Glazed Pork with Sweet Potatoes, 18
Pan-Roasted Chicken & Vegetables, 15
Puff Pastry Chicken Potpie, 35
Seafood Casserole, 38
Sunday Roast Chicken, 21
Turkey Sausage-Stuffed Acorn Squash, 16
Vegetable & Beef Stuffed Red Peppers, 23

PASTA & NOODLES
Alfredo-Pancetta Stuffed Shells, 12
Artichoke Florentine Pasta, 18
Couscous Meatball Soup, 74
Festive Slow-Cooked Beef Tips, 22
Fried Prosciutto Tortellini, 106
Grandma's Cajun Chicken & Spaghetti, 23
Light & Lemony Scampi, 20
Slow Cooker Bacon Mac & Cheese, 64
Slow Cooker Turkey Pesto Lasagna, 11
Summer Orzo, 61
The Ultimate Chicken Noodle Soup, 70
Turkey Alfredo Tetrazzini, 29

PEAS
Fresh Sugar Snap Pea Salad, 48
Split Pea Soup with Ham & Jalapeno, 76

PEPPERS
Confetti Corn Bread, 76
Red & Green Salad with Toasted Almonds, 45
Split Pea Soup with Ham & Jalapeno, 76
Sweet & Spicy Jalapeno Poppers, 100
Vegetable & Beef Stuffed Red Peppers, 23

PIES & TARTS
Blueberry, Basil & Goat Cheese Pie, 90
Chocolate S'mores Tart, 87
Easy Lemon Pie, 84

POPPY SEEDS
Spinach Salad with Poppy Seed Dressing, 50
Tangy Poppy Seed Fruit Salad, 48

PORK
(also see Bacon & Pancetta; Ham,
Canadian Bacon & Prosciutto; Sausage &
Pepperoni)
Apple-Cherry Pork Medallions, 7
Baked Chops & Fries, 35
Country Ribs Dinner, 9
Orange-Glazed Pork with Sweet Potatoes, 18

POTATOES & FRIES
Baked Baby Potatoes with Olive Pesto, 102
Baked Chops & Fries, 35
Beef Potato Meat Loaf, 9
Butternut Squash & Potato Mash, 56
Country Ribs Dinner, 9

Cream Cheese Mashed Potatoes, 64
Creamy Chicken & Broccoli Stew, 71
Grilled Firecracker Potato Salad, 53
Roasted Tater Rounds with Green Onions &
   Tarragon, 61
Scalloped Potatoes with Mushrooms, 62
You're-Bacon-Me-Crazy Potato Salad, 43

PUFF PASTRY
Puff Pastry Chicken Potpie, 35

QUICK BREADS & MUFFINS
Garlic Bread Mini Muffins, 75
Olive & Onion Quick Bread, 78
Roasted Butternut Squash Bread, 71
Sesame Herb Pull-Apart Bread, 74

QUINOA
Avocado & Chickpea Quinoa Salad, 43

RADISHES
Orange-Glazed Carrots, Onions &
   Radishes, 66
Ravishing Radish Salad, 47

RASPBERRIES
Chocolate-Raspberry Whoopie Pies, 90
Refreshing Raspberry Iced Tea, 105

RICE
Almond Turkey Casserole, 30
Apple-Cherry Pork Medallions, 7
Baked Orange Roughy & Rice, 33
Hot Chicken Casserole, 25
Seafood Casserole, 38
Slow Cooker Spinach & Rice, 55

ROLLS
Cheese-Filled Garlic Rolls, 81
Cornmeal Dinner Rolls, 73
Honey-Squash Dinner Rolls, 78

SALADS
BEAN SALADS
Avocado & Chickpea Quinoa Salad, 43
Vibrant Black-Eyed Pea Salad, 47
FRUIT SALADS
German Apples, 46
Juicy Watermelon Salad, 41
Roasted Apple Salad with Spicy Maple-Cider
   Vinaigrette, 52
Tangy Poppy Seed Fruit Salad, 48
GREEN SALADS
Company Green Salad, 48
Red & Green Salad with Toasted Almonds, 45
Spinach Salad with Poppy Seed Dressing, 50
MISCELLANEOUS SALADS
Blue Cheese Apple Slaw, 49
Southern Corn Bread Salad, 53
POTATO SALADS
Grilled Firecracker Potato Salad, 53
You're-Bacon-Me-Crazy Potato Salad, 43
VEGETABLE SALADS
Balsamic Cucumber Salad, 49
Beet Salad with Lemon Dressing, 52

Alphabetical Index